# More Praise for bell

## Salvation: Black Pec

"When truth teller and careful writer bell hooks offers a book, I like to be standing at the bookshop when it opens. I know I will buy copies for my family and friends and even the odd stranger who I think needs to read books."
—Maya Angelou

"Hooks offers one of her most touching and tender books to date in *Salvation*. . . . [She] offers chapters on Black love that will conjure familiar memories that are warm and inviting."
—*Essence*

"An impassioned plea. . . . [Hooks has a] flair for crisp writing. . . . Stinging arguments. . . . Hooks reaches beyond the theoretical to address various walks of black life."
—*Publishers Weekly*

"A frank and hard-hitting, psychologically astute, and beautifully crafted treatise on the meaning of love and why it's essential to a healthy society. . . . Readers of every hue will benefit from hooks's piercing insights into the troubled state of our collective soul and find solace in her belief that 'love is our hope and salvation.'"
—*Booklist*

"A manual for fixing our culture. . . . In writing that is elegant and penetratingly simple, [hooks] gives voice to some things we may know in our hearts but need an interpreter like her to help process. One of the book's major contributions . . . is its probing analysis of how the mass media—entertainment and news—help to shape what we think about ourselves and what others think of us."
—*Black Issues Book Review*

## All About Love: New Visions

"It is a warm affirmation that love is possible and an attack on the culture of narcissism and selfishness."
—*The New York Times Book Review*

"A gracefully written volume . . . her treatise offers a deeply personal—and in this age of chicken-soupy psychobabble—unabashedly honest view of relationships." —*Entertainment Weekly*

"Every page offers useful nuggets of wisdom to aid the reader in overcoming the fears of total intimacy and of loss. . . . Hooks's view of amour is ultimately a pleasing, upbeat alternative to the slew of books that proclaim the demise of love in our cynical time."
—*Publishers Weekly*

"*All About Love: New Visions* promises to be one of the most engaging, life-affirming reads of the year. Come to it with an open mind, and an open heart, and prepare to be transformed."
—*Black Issues Book Review*

"A spiritual handbook, weighty with platitudes, yet refreshed with some thoughtful analyses that offer seekers a way to explore love's meaning, or meaningless[ness]." —*Kirkus Reviews*

"Her vision seems idealistic . . . ambitious. Yet it touches a yearning we all have and is expressed so sincerely . . . [that] hooks's *New Visions* reminds us that we can be a part of a loving community."
—*Philadelphia Inquirer*

"Pay attention to bell hooks. The American writer and cultural critic is becoming a household word . . . hooks's writing typically inspires, enlightens, and provokes. She is an academic wild card, the brilliant feminist whose sharp mind can slice the latest scholarly shibboleth."
—*Boston Globe and Mail*

"She provides a refreshing spiritual treatise that steps outside the confines of the intellect and into the wilds of the heart."
—*Seattle Weekly*

"Like love, this book is worth the commitment." —*Toronto Sun*

Marion Ettlinger

# About the Author

BELL HOOKS is a cultural critic, feminist theorist, scholar, and writer. Born and raised in Hopkinsville, Kentucky, hooks received her B.A. from Stanford University, her M.A. from the University of Wisconsin, and her Ph.D. from the University of California at Santa Cruz. Celebrated as one of our nation's leading public intellectuals by *The Atlantic Monthly*, and named one of *Utne Reader*'s "100 Visionaries Who Could Change Your Life," hooks is a charismatic speaker who divides her time among teaching, writing, and lecturing around the world.

Hooks has served as professor in the English departments at Yale University, Oberlin College, and, most recently, as distinguished Professor of English at City College and the Graduate Center of the City University of New York. She is the author of twenty books, including *Ain't I a Woman*, which *Publishers Weekly* named one of the twenty most influential women's books of the last twenty years. She lives in New York City.

Also by bell hooks

# Salvation

## Black People and Love

## *bell hooks*

HARPER  PERENNIAL

A hardcover edition of this book was published in 2001 by William Morrow, an imprint of HarperCollins Publishers.

HarperCollins books may be purchased for educational, business, or sales promotional use. For information, please e-mail the Special Markets Department at SPsales @harpercollins.com.

First Perennial edition published 2001.

*Designed by JAM Design*

The Library of Congress has catalogued the hardcover edition as follows:

Hooks, Bell.
    Salvation: Black people and love / bell hooks.—1st ed.
    p. cm.
    ISBN 0-06-018494-9 (alk. paper)
      1. Afro-Americans—Social life and customs. 2. Afro-Americans—Social conditions. 3. Afro-Americans—Psychology. 4. Love—United States. 5. Man-woman relationships—United States. 6. Friendship—United States. I. Title.

E185.86 .H739 2001
306.7'089'96073—dc21

00-061648

ISBN 0-06-095949-5 (pbk.)

23 CPI 37

Printed by CPI Group (UK) Ltd, Croydon CR0 4YY

anthony, the first love letter I ever wrote was sent to you. it included this quote from Malcolm X: "We ourselves have to lift the level of our community, take the standards of our community to a higher level, make our own society beautiful so that we will be satisfied . . . we've got to change our own minds about each other. we have to see each other with new eyes . . . we have to come together with warmth . . ."

celebrating ten years—the warmth you bring to my life—all praise

Salvation is being on the right road, not having reached a destination.

—Martin Luther King Jr.

One tries to recover, to be once more in good shape, to become whole again. . . . And I think that is the beginning of awakening. People speak about sudden enlightenment. It is not something very difficult to understand; each of us has undergone that kind of experience in our own life. The distance separating forgetfulness, ignorance, and enlightenment—that distance is short; it is so short it is no distance at all. One may be ignorant now, but he can be enlightened in the next second. The recovering of oneself can be realized in just one portion of one second. And to be aware of who we are, what we are, what we are doing, what we are thinking, seems to be a very easy thing to do—and yet it is the most important thing; to remember—the starting point of the salvation of oneself.

—THICH NHAT HANH,
*The Raft Is Not the Shore*

# Contents

CONTENTS

# love is our hope

LOVE AND DEATH were the great mysteries of my childhood. When I did not feel loved, I wanted to die. Death would take away the trauma of feeling unwanted, out of place, of always being the one who does not fit in. I knew then that love gave life meaning. But it disturbed me that nothing I heard about love fit with the world around me. At church we learned that love was peaceful, kind, forgiving, redemptive, faithful. And yet everybody seemed troubled in their relationships. Even as a child I pondered the gap between what folks said about love and the ways they behaved.

As a young woman hoping to find love, I was disappointed in the relationships I witnessed and troubled by

my own efforts. Even though I was coming into womanhood at a time of free love and open marriage, I dreamed
of being with a partner for a lifetime. My visions of marriage had been shaped by the relationship between my
maternal grandmother and grandfather, who had been
together for more than seventy-five years. An essay I wrote
about their relationship titled "inspired eccentricity"
described how different they were, and yet there was in
their relationship what therapist Fred Newman calls "radical acceptance." They had the curious blend of together-
ness and autonomy that is needed in healthy relationships
but difficult to find. I have not found it, even though I keep
searching.

From my college days to the present, most folks I
encounter consider it foolish and naive of anyone to want
to spend a lifetime with a partner. Again and again they
point to divorce rates and continual breakups among gay
and straight couples as signs that spending a lifetime with
someone is just not a realistic desire. Cynically, many of
them believe that couples who remain together for more
than twenty years are usually unhappy or just coexisting.
That's certainly true of many marriages (my parents have
been together for almost fifty years but have not managed
to create a happy household). But there are couples who
find it sheer bliss to be spending a lifetime with one
another. Their bonds are just as emblematic of what is

real and possible as the reality of ruptured and broken bonds.

I learned from watching my grandparents that sustained joyous commitment in a relationship does not mean that there are no down and difficult times. In my first book on love, *all about love: new visions,* I continually state that love does not bring an end to difficulties, it gives us the strength to cope with difficulties in a constructive way. That book, like this one, is dedicated to Anthony, with whom I have had (and continue to have) long discussions about the nature of love. A thirty-something guy whose parents separated when he was a boy, he has no vision of a relationship lasting for a lifetime. In fact the idea seems "weird" to him. Only by experience is he learning to trust that lasting bonds are to be cherished and valued.

All love relationships flourish when there is sustained commitment. Constancy in the midst of change strengthens bonds. In both romantic relationships and friendships, I enjoy going through changes with loved ones, watching how we develop. To me it's similar to the delight and awe that loving parents feel as they witness children go through myriad changes. Having a longtime partner who both participates in our growth while also bearing witness is one of love's profound pleasures. I celebrate lasting love in *all about love: new visions,* a work that generally discusses the meaning of love in our culture and what we should know about love.

Lecturing in public schools during my tour for that book, I was continually distressed to hear black children of all ages express their deep conviction that love does not exist. Time and time again I was shaken to my core hearing young black folks emphatically state, "There is no such thing as love." In *all about love,* I define love as a combination of care, knowledge, responsibility, respect, trust, and commitment. Calling out the extent to which our nation has become cynical about love, it should have come as no surprise that the pervasive lovelessness I talk about is not only most deeply felt in the hearts of children but that it would be among those groups of children, black girls and boys, who are collectively disenfranchised, neglected, or rendered invisible in this society, and that I would hear these sentiments frankly acknowledged. When asked about anti-racist struggle by white critics who did not understand the need for militant protest, playwright Lorraine Hansberry often replied that "the acceptance of our present condition is the only form of extremism which discredits us before our children." Standing before black children who tell me there is no love in clear, flat, dispassionate voices, I confront our collective failure as a nation, and as African-Americans, to create a world where we can all know love. This book is a response to this crisis of lovelessness. It dares us to courageously create the love our children need to be whole, to live fully and well.

Early on in our nation's history, when white settlers colonized Africans through systems of indentured labor and slavery, they justified these acts of racial aggression by claiming that black people were not fully human. In particular it was in relation to matters of the heart, of care and love, that the colonizers drew examples to prove that black folk were dehumanized, that we lacked the range of emotions accepted as a norm among civilized folk. In the racist mindset the enslaved African was incapable of deep feeling and fine emotions. Since love was considered to be a finer sentiment, black folks were seen as lacking the capacity to love.

When slavery ended, many of the racist stereotypes that had been used to subordinate and alienate black people were challenged. But the question of whether or not black people were capable of love, of deep and complex emotions, continued to be a subject for heated discussion and debate. In the early 1900s, black scholars began to debate the issue of whether or not the dehumanizing impact of racist terrorism and abuse had left black people crippled when it came to the matter of love. Writers like Richard Wright, Zora Neale Hurston, Ann Petry, Lorraine Hansberry, and James Baldwin sustained vibrant debates about the issue of love in fiction and nonfiction.

Hurston's novel *Their Eyes Were Watching God* showed

that love was not only possible among the poor and oppressed but a necessary and essential life force. In her provocative protest novel *The Street,* Ann Petry offered the world an image of black heterosexual love where black men betray black women through sexual objectification and manipulation. Opportunistic greed leads the black male hero to assault and disrespect the integrity of the black female who loves him. Wright offered to the world in his protest novel *Native Son* an image of blackness that made it synonymous with dehumanization, with the absence of feeling. His character Bigger Thomas embodied a lovelessness so relentless it struck a chord of terror in the minds of black activists who had been struggling to counter similar images of blackness emerging from the white imagination.

In his autobiography, *Black Boy,* Wright dared to tell the world that he believed dehumanization had happened to many black folks, that ongoing racist genocide had left us damaged, forever wounded in the space where we would know love. His critics Baldwin and Hansberry challenged this one-dimensional image of blackness. In *Nobody Knows My Name,* Baldwin declared: "I suggest that the role of the Negro in American life has something to do with our concept of what God is.... To be with God is really to be involved with some enormous, overwhelming desire, and joy, and power which you cannot control, which controls you. I conceive of my own life as a journey toward something I did not understand, which in the going toward, makes me better. I conceive of God, in fact, as a means of liberation and not a means to control others. Love does not begin and end the way we seem to think it does. Love is a battle, love is a war; love is a growing up. No one in the world . . . knows more—knows Americans better or . . . loves them more than the American Negro." In the mid-sixties, Hansberry told a group of aspiring young black writers that if they wanted to understand the meaning of love, they should talk to black folks and "ask the troubadors who come from those who have loved when all reason pointed to the uselessness and foolhardiness of love." Daringly she stated: "Perhaps we shall be the teachers when it is done. Out of the depths of pain we have thought to be our sole heritage in this world—O, we know about love!" Both Baldwin and Hansberry believed that black identity was forged in triumphant struggle to resist dehumanization, that the choice to love was a necessary dimension of liberation.

As late as 1974, writer June Jordan published the essay "Notes Toward a Black Balancing of Love and Hatred," discussing the issue of which was the definitive black experience, the triumph of love over dehumanization celebrated in Hurston's work or the triumph of violence, self-hatred, and destruction depicted in Wright's *Native*

*Son.* Jordan states: "Unquestionably, *Their Eyes Were Watching God* is the prototypical Black novel of affirmation; it is the most successful and convincing and exemplary novel of Black love that we have, period." Yet Jordan urges us to feel no need to choose between Hurston or Wright, for she believes that in his dehumanization Bigger Thomas "teaches as much about the necessity of love, of being able to love without being destroyed, as Hurston's Janie Starks," and declares that "we should equally value and equally emulate Black Protest and Black Affirmation, for we require both." Despite this prophetic insight, in the world of anti-racist activism a call to violence rather than a call to love had already become the order of the day. The affirmation and love Jordan deemed essential was already under siege.

Even though prophets of civil rights had always emphasized a liberation theology that upheld love as essential both to the creation in black folks of a healthy self-esteem undergirding resistance struggle and to the humanizing of hard hearted white folks, this focus on love did not prevail. As an organized black liberation movement emphasizing love was replaced by a call for militant violent resistance, the value of love in movements for black self-determination and liberation was no longer highlighted. When the seventies came to an end, a new cynicism had become the order of the day. The ethic of love once evoked by visionary leaders as the fundamental source of power and strength of our freedom struggle began to have little or no meaning in the lives of black folks, especially young people.

Indeed, love was mocked—not just the love-your-enemies message of nonviolent revolution spearheaded by Martin Luther King, but also the message of building self-love, healthy self-esteem, and loving communities. As the quest for power subsumed the quest for liberation in anti-racist struggle, there was little or no discussion of the purpose and meaning of love in black experience, of love in liberation struggle. The abandonment of a discourse on love, of strategies to create a foundation of self-esteem and self-worth that would undergird struggles for self-determination, laid the groundwork for the undermining of all our efforts to create a society where blackness could be loved, by black folks, by everyone.

The denigration of love in black experience, across classes, has become the breeding ground for nihilism, for despair, for ongoing terroristic violence and predatory opportunism. It has taken from many black people the positive agency needed if we are to collectively self-actualize and be self-determining. Many of the material gains generated by militant anti-racist struggle have had little positive impact on the psyches and souls of black folks, for the revolution from within that is the foundation on which we build self-love and love of others has not taken place.

Black folks and our allies in struggle who care about the fate of Black America recognize that the transformative power of love in daily life is the only force that can solve the myriad crises we now face.

We cannot effectively resist domination if our efforts to create meaningful, lasting personal and social change are not grounded in a love ethic. Prophetically, *Salvation: Black People and Love* calls us to return to love. Addressing the meaning of love in black experience today, calling for a return to an ethic of love as the platform on which to renew progressive anti-racist struggle, and offering a blueprint for black survival and self-determination, this work courageously takes us to the heart of the matter. To give ourselves love, to love blackness, is to restore the true meaning of freedom, hope, and possibility in all our lives.

When black children tell me, "There is no love," I tell them love is always there—that nothing can keep us from love if we dare to seek it and to treasure what we find. Even when we cannot change ongoing exploitation and domination, love gives life meaning, purpose, and direction. Doing the work of love, we ensure our survival and our triumph over the forces of evil and destruction. Hansberry was right to insist that "we know about love." But many of us have forgotten what we know, what love is or why we need love to sustain life. This book reminds us. Love is our hope and our salvation.

Love takes off the masks that we fear we cannot live without and know we cannot live within. I use the word *love* here not merely in the personal sense but as a state of being, or a state of grace—not in the infantile American sense of being made happy but in the tough and universal sense of quest and daring and growth.

— JAMES BALDWIN,
*The Fire Next Time*

# Salvation

*One*

# the heart of the matter

EVERY NOW AND then I return to poor black communities I lived in or visited during my childhood. These neighborhoods that were once vibrant, full of life, with flowers planted outside the walls of run-down shacks, folks on the porch, are now barren landscapes. Many of them look like war zones. Returning, I bear witness to desolation. Surrounded by an aura of emptiness, these places, once shrouded in hope, now stand like barren arms, lonely and empty. No one moves into their embrace to touch, to be held and to hold, to comfort. Poverty has not created this desolation; the generations of folks who inhabited these landscapes have always been poor. What I witness are ravages of the spirit, the debris left after emotional assault and explosion. What I witness is heart-wrenching loss, despair, and a lovelessness so profound it alters the nature of environments both inside and out.

The desolation of these places where love was and is now gone is just one among many signs of the ongoing crisis of spirit that ravages black people and black communities everywhere. More often than not this crisis of spirit is talked about by political leaders and community organizers as engendered by life-threatening poverty, violence, or the ravages of addiction. While it is utterly true that all these forces undermine our capacity to be well, underlying these issues is a profound spiritual crisis. As a people we are losing heart. Our collective crisis is as much an emotional one as a material one. It cannot be healed simply by money. We know this because so many of the leaders who preach to us about the necessity of gaining material privilege, who are holders of wealth and status, are as lost, as disenabled emotionally, as those among us who lack material well-being. Leaders who are addicted to alcohol, shopping, violence, or gaining power and fame by any means necessary rarely offer to anyone a vision of emotional well-being that can heal and restore broken lives and broken communities.

To heal our wounded communities, which are diverse and multilayered, we must return to a love ethic, one that is exemplified by the combined forces of care, respect, knowledge, and responsibility. Throughout our history in this nation black leaders have spoken about the importance of love. Indeed, now and then contemporary leaders stress the importance of a love ethic. Referring to the love ethic in his work *Race Matters,* philosopher Cornel West contends: "A love ethic has nothing to do with sentimental feelings or tribal connections. . . . Self-love and love of others are both modes toward increasing self-valuation and encouraging political resistance in one's community." While contemporary black leaders and thinkers talk about the need to have a love ethic as the foundation of struggles for black self-determination, in actuality most nonfiction writing about black experience does not address the issue of love in an extensive manner.

Since our leaders and scholars agree that one measure of the crisis black people are experiencing is lovelessness, it should be evident that we need a body of literature, both sociological and psychological work, addressing the issue of love among black people, its relevance to political struggle, its meaning in our private lives. I began thinking about the lack of commentary on love in black life when the debate about separate schools for black boys was taking place. Everywhere I turned, I kept hearing that black boys needed discipline, that they needed to learn the meaning of hard work, that they needed to have strong role models who would set boundaries for them and teach obedience.

Again and again a militaristic model of boot camp and basic training was presented as a solution to the behavior problems of young black men. Not once did I hear anyone speak about black boys needing love as a foundation that would ensure the development of sound self-esteem, self-love, and love of others. Even though black male leaders were among the voices defining lovelessness as a key cause of hopelessness and despair among black youth, none of them talked about the role of love in the education of young black boys.

When huge numbers of black males, young and old, gathered in the nation's capital for the Million Man March, there was no discussion of love. The word "love" was not evoked by any prominent speaker. Again and again when we talk about the contemporary crisis in black life, discussions of love are absent. This has not always been the case. Throughout our history in this country, radical black political leadership has emerged from religious settings, whether they be Christian, Islamic, or less recognized spiritual paths. Within these religions, especially Christianity, love has been central.

The Reverend Martin Luther King Jr. was a prophet of love preaching to the souls of black folks and our non-white allies in struggles everywhere. His collection of sermons *Strength to Love* was first published in 1963. Later, in 1967, in an address to a group of antiwar clergy, he stated: "When I speak of love I am not speaking of some sentimental and weak response. I am speaking of that force which all of the great religions have seen as the supreme unifying principle of life. Love is somehow the key that unlocks the door which leads to ultimate reality. This Hindu-Moslem-Christian-Jewish-Buddhist belief about ultimate reality is beautifully summed up in the first epistle of Saint John: 'Let us love one another, for love is God and everyone that loveth is both of God and knoweth God.' " Much of King's focus on love as the fundamental principle that should guide the freedom struggle was directed toward upholding his belief in nonviolence. While he admonished black people again and again to recognize the importance of loving our enemies, of not hating white people, he did not give as much attention to the issue of self-love and communal love among black people.

One of the most talked about sermons in the collection was titled "Loving Your Enemies." King used this sermon to explain and justify his urging black people to love our enemies: "While we abhor segregation, we shall love the segregationist. This is the only way to create the beloved community." Yet he also spoke directly to the white majority, stating: "To our most bitter opponents we say: 'We shall match your capacity to inflict suffering by our capacity to endure suffering. We shall meet your physical force with soul force. Do to us what you will, and we shall continue to love you. We cannot in all good conscience obey your unjust laws, because non-cooperation with evil is as much a moral obligation as is cooperation with good. Throw us in jail, and we shall still love you. Send your hooded perpetrators of violence into our community at the midnight hour and beat us and leave us half dead, and we shall still love you." Nothing was said in this collection about loving blackness. King did not address the issue of how black people would love the enemy if they did not love themselves.

This emphasis on black people loving our enemies was the aspect of King's political agenda most criticized by radicals approaching black liberation from a more militant standpoint. Again and again Malcolm X warned against this message of nonviolence. In his 1964 speech to southern black youth, he told them: "Don't you run around here trying to make friends with somebody who's depriving you of your rights. They're not your friends, no, they're your enemies. . . . I'm not going to let somebody who hates me tell me to love him." On those rare occasions when Malcolm X spoke about love, he addressed the need for black folks to change how we saw one another, calling attention to internalized racist thinking. Overall, though, he did not have much to say on the subject of love.

Underlying his attacks and the critiques of other militant black leaders on King's philosophy of nonviolence was the assumption that love was for the weak and faint of heart. Real men attended to more important matters. Militant black power leaders who took up the mantle of black self-determination, folks like Huey Newton, Elaine Brown, and Kwame Toure (then known as Stokely Carmichael), preferred discussions that centered on building healthy self-esteem rather than discussions of love. More and more, as black radicalism was divorced from its religious roots, becoming more secular, discussions of love were silenced. Increasingly, as black liberation was made synonymous with the creation of strong black patriarchs, love could no longer have a central place in the movement. Real men were fighters, not lovers. Freedom, militant black leaders, told the world, was about the will to power and not the will to love.

The more freedom became synonymous with gaining equal rights within the existing social structure, the less love was a part of this equation. Gaining access to material privilege increasingly became the emphasis of the black liberation struggle. Economic self-sufficiency was defined as the sole measure of freedom. In this way black political leaders who were more aggressive and militant, who advocated violence, actually did not have as radical an agenda as the one King set forth in his writings. Their insistence on violent struggle was not to change the existing social order but rather to gain power and privilege within the system. In several sermons in *Strength to Love*, King warned against the potential evils of capitalism, calling attention to the danger of loving money more than freedom. Unequivocally he stated: "I still contend that the love of money is the root of much evil and may cause a man to become a gross materialist." Of course King had no idea that black folks would one day gain access to material wealth by exploiting blackness in ways similar to those of the dominant culture. Yet in speeches and sermons delivered shortly before he was assassinated (many of them collected in the anthology *A Testament of Hope*) he vehemently opposed imperialism, militarism, and capitalism, calling for radical transformation of society.

With prophetic insight, King realized that a love ethic was central to any meaningful challenge to domination. In his last works, he was concerned less with teaching black people to love our enemies than with the threat of moral corruption posed by our embracing of materialistic hedonism, which he believed would create a spiritual crisis for the nation. His vision was prescient. Describing the current plight of black people in *Prophetic Reflections,* Cornel West states: "There is increasing class division and differentiation, creating on the one hand a significant black middle class, highly anxiety-ridden, insecure, willing to be co-opted and incorporated into the powers that be, concerned with racism to the degree that it poses constraints on social mobility; and, on the other, a vast and growing black underclass that embodies a kind of walking nihilism of pervasive drug addiction, pervasive homicide, and an exponential rise in suicide. Now, because of deindustrialization, we also have a devastated black industrial working class. We are talking here about tremendous hopelessness." West does not even mention the growing number of black elites, wealthy individuals who have unprecedented access to mass media, who as producers and shapers of culture promote values detrimental to the collective survival of black people. To protect their class interests, these individuals often make it seem as though black capitalism is the same as black self-determination. By embracing and projecting liberal individualism as the only way to success, they undermine a vision of collective well-being that necessarily requires sharing skills and resources.

More than any other individuals, wealthy black people have by words and deeds encouraged the black masses to worship at the throne of money. Addiction to materialism knows no class. Yet the impact of this addiction differs depending on one's class. A rich black entertainer in sports or the music industry buying fancy cars, designer clothes, drugs, and so on need not prey upon others. Yet poor and underclass black folks who turn to selling drugs as a means of acquiring material luxuries prey upon the members of their communities. When a rich black person is addicted to drugs or alcohol, he or she has easy access to a therapeutic world that can offer help and assistance. Poor and down-trodden black folks who are substance abusers often have no recourse. Their attempts to imitate the lifestyles of the rich and famous usually have tragic consequences.

No matter what our class, black people who worship money are not interested in a love ethic. Striving for eco-nomic self-sufficiency is a worthy and necessary goal for everyone. Being economically in control of one's resources is an important aspect of healthy self-esteem. Valuing material goods above all else creates spiritual crisis. This crisis was vividly dramatized in Lorraine Hansberry's award-winning play *A Raisin in the Sun*. After the death of the father, Big Walter, the Younger family must decide what to do with the insurance money they receive. The adult son, Walter Lee, wants to use the money to open a liquor store. His mother, Lena, confronts him and asks, "Since when did money become life?" Written at the end of the fifties, this play exemplified the transition black peo-ple were making as we gained greater social mobility. Non-market values of communalism and sharing of resources, symbolized by the extended family household, were being replaced by liberal individualism. Walter Lee is not concerned about the good of the whole community; he wants capitalist success for himself. When Lena warns against the selling of an abusive substance, he mocks her.

Prophetically, Hansberry foresaw the negative impact worship of money and acceptance of addiction would have on black life. In her play, nonmarket values prevail. Yet they have not prevailed in the lives of many black people. Hansberry never mentions love in *A Raisin in the Sun*. Yet she was critical of the undue emphasis placed on attaining material success in her family and in black life in general, believing we neglected to focus on love to our detriment. In autobiographical work she describes her family: "Of love and my parents there is little to be written: their relationship to their children was utilitarian. We were fed and housed and dressed and outfitted with more cash than our associates and that was all. We were not a loving people." She recognized that the world she was raised in was one where material success was all that mattered.

In Hansberry's day there was an ongoing discussion about whether or not the dehumanizing impact of racism had in fact made it impossible for black people to love. Her beloved friend and comrade James Baldwin was often at the forefront of these debates. His quarrels with fellow novelist Richard Wright often centered on the issue of dehumanization. Wright believed wholeheartedly that black people were incapable of loving because of the emotional scars inflicted by racist oppression. Wisely, Baldwin insisted that we are always more than our pain. Not only did he believe in our capacity to love, he felt black people were uniquely situated to risk loving because we had suffered. In his essay "The Fire Next Time," he writes of black people's "spiritual resilience": "I do not mean to be sentimental about suffering . . . but people who cannot suffer can never grow up, can never discover who they are." Baldwin would no doubt be shocked to see that many black people today do not bear suffering in a way that makes them follow a path to love. Instead, pervasive addiction means that the desire to numb pain is greater than the force of spirit that would lead us to journey through pain and find our way to healing. In the essay "Where Is the Love," June Jordan reminds us that "it is always the love, whether we look to the spirit of Fannie Lou Hamer or the spirit of Agostinho Neto, it is always the love that will carry action into positive new places."

Love remains for black people a crucial path to healing. In retrospect it is clear that if we do not create a foundation of love on which to build our struggles for freedom and self-determination, forces of evil, of greed, and of corruption undermine and ultimately destroy all our efforts. It is not too late for black people to return to love, to ask again the metaphysical questions commonly raised by black artists and thinkers during the heyday of freedom struggles, questions about the relationship between dehumanization and our capacity to love, questions about internalized racism and self-hatred.

Contemporary focus on material gain as the key to healing our crisis has deflected attention away from the need
for emotional growth, for us to embrace more wholeheartedly the art and act of loving. Tina Turner's hit song
"What's Love Got to Do with It" gave popular expression
to the turning away from a love ethic. Much hip-hop culture promotes hedonistic materialism, making everything
associated with gaining wealth embody the essence of
cool. Like the culture as a whole, masses of black people
now look to material success as the sole measure of value
and meaning in life. While we do not need to love in order
to attain great riches, without a sound emotional foundation material privilege easily corrupts. Gaining access to
material privilege will never satisfy needs of the spirit.
Those hungers persist and haunt us. We seek to satisfy
those cravings by endless consumption, appetites that easily turn into addictions that can never be satisfied. Needs
of the spirit can only be satisfied when we care for the
soul. Our ancestors knew this. Only a politics of conversion where we return to love can save us.

Letting all black people and the world know we cannot
live by goods alone is crucial to our collective survival and
well-being. We have been wounded in the place where we
would know love. We know this. The lovelessness that
abounds in black life, cutting across class and circumstance, stands as testimony. Addressing love, we proclaim

our full and complex humanity. Martin Luther King urged us to remember that "love transforms with redemptive power." To return to love, making it a central issue in our efforts for collective recovery and healing is not a move away from political action. Unless love is the force undergirding our efforts to transform society, we lose our way.

Writing about the way militant black power activism began to move in a direction that was anti-love, Julius Lester shared this powerful insight in a column for *The Guardian:* "Our love for black people was overwhelmed by our inability to do everything to make that love manifest, and after a while we could not even love each other." Lester recalls in an essay about the sixties that "the Movement disappointed us and we disappointed ourselves." He shares the powerful insight that had black liberation struggle remained true to a love ethic, its positive impact would have been more profound and lasting. Recalling this period, Maya Angelou stresses that it was not a time when black folk were turning away from domination toward love. Instead, she writes, "Black men talk about change where what they really mean . . . is exchange. They want to take over the positions of power white men have." Without changing structures of domination, we leave in place the culture of lovelessness.

Love is profoundly political. Our deepest revolution will come when we understand this truth. Only love can

give us the strength to go forward in the midst of heart-
break and misery. Only love can give us the power to reconcile, to redeem, the power to renew weary spirits and
save lost souls. The transformative power of love is the
foundation of all meaningful social change. Without love
our lives are without meaning. Love is the heart of the
matter. When all else has fallen away, love sustains.

*Two*

# we wear the mask

IN THE DIASPORA, most black people's relationship to love has been shaped by the trauma of abandonment. Whether we take as the foundation of our psycho history the African explorers who came to the so-called New World before Columbus, the free individuals who came in small numbers as immigrants, or the large population of black people who were enslaved and brought here against their will, this is an emotional backdrop full of the drama of union and reunion, of loss and abandonment. It has always struck me as particularly meaningful that the first Africans who came to these shores fellowshiped with the indigenous people they met here, sharing resources and knowledge, but ultimately chose to return home. They valued the culture and connections they had left behind more than anything they found in the New World. In this way they were no different from the Spanish colonizers who would travel in their wake. They chose to come and they chose to leave. When this history of power, freedom, and choice is juxtaposed against the legacy of powerlessness, enslavement, and absence of choice, a complex emotional backdrop unfolds.

For way too long, black people in this society were taught only that we came to this country as slaves. It has taken years of progressive anti-racist struggle to create enough cultural momentum so that a holistic picture of our history in this nation, a true, complete vision of our past, one that is not tainted by racist biases, can emerge. Whatever its flaws and defects, the movie *Amistad* and all the publicity it received globally reminded the world that all black people did not come here as slaves. Who we are as African-Americans, as black folks in the diaspora, our cultural destiny, has been shaped by both the enslaved and the free.

Autobiographies and biographies of enslaved black people tell a collective story of individuals emotionally ravaged by separation from homeland, clan, and family. Naturally, these stories say little about love and tell us more about the nature of human suffering and heartache. In his insightful work *The Art of Loving*, Erich Fromm

SALVATION

defines love as a fusion of care, respect, knowledge, and responsibility. Drawing upon this work and adding to it, M. Scott Peck extends this definition to include "the will to nurture one's own and another's spiritual growth." With this understanding of love's meaning it is clear that more often than not slavery made it all but impossible for black people to love one another. When emotional ties were established between individuals, when children were born to enslaved mothers and fathers, these attachments were often severed. No matter the tenderness of connection, it was often overshadowed by the trauma of abandonment and loss.

Slave narratives document the efforts individual black people made to normalize life in an abnormal circumstance. Despite the dehumanization enacted by the dominant culture of white supremacy, with spiritual resiliency enslaved black people worked to create a subculture where bonds of affection could be forged and sustained. Two of the most widely read slave narratives, by Frederick Douglass and Harriet Jacobs, share detailed memories of the psychological tension generated by the conditions of enslavement. In Jacobs's narrative she tells of a moment when her older brother Willie is torn between family bonds and the demands of enslavement: "One day, when his father and his mistress both happened to call him at the same time, he hesitated between the two; being perplexed

to know which had the strongest claim upon his obedience. He finally concluded to go to his mistress." Douglass
insisted in his narrative that "he had never known a
mother's love," but he shared at the beginning of his story
that his mother had walked miles to hold him as a child
even though she risked brutal punishment.

To Douglass, a mother's love was defined by care that
was sustained, that could be counted on. In his case the
trauma of separation and abandonment overwhelmed
these early memories of loving care. Jacobs was cared for
deeply by her grandmother. That care lasted throughout
her lifetime. Finally escaping slavery, Jacobs wrote: "How
that faithful, loving old heart would leap for joy, if she
could look on me and my children now that we were
freed!" Importantly, Jacobs concluded her narrative with
this declaration: "Reader, my story ends with freedom; not
in the usual way, with marriage. I and my children are now
free! We are as free from the power of slaveholders as are
the white people of the north; and though that, according
to my ideas, is not saying a great deal, it is a vast improve-
ment in *my* condition. The dream of my life is not yet realized. I do not sit with my children in a home of my own. I
still long for a hearthstone of my own, however humble. I
wish it for my children's sake far more than my own."
Like so many other black folks who made the transition
from slavery to freedom but who were still compelled by

economic circumstances to spend most of their time living with and working for whites, Jacobs longed to give her children sustained emotional care and was not always able to give them the love she knew they needed and deserved.

From slavery until the present day, black folks have felt conflicting tensions between survival needs and the demands of the heart. No doubt this is in part why historian Leon Litwack titled his book about the lives of southern black people in the age of Jim Crow *Trouble in Mind*. Survival in a racist society often dictated that black people adjust to values and social mores imposed on us by the white world, which often affected our capacity to be loving. Chronicles of life after slavery and on into the mid-1900s show that black children were often given mixed messages by parents. They would be told by parents to respect themselves and other people, to cultivate good manners, to tell the truth, only to then be compelled by these same elders to act in a different way when encountering the white power structure.

Litwack's book is full of testimony about the confusion black children faced as they tried to live within a world that had two codes of behavior. Many southern black people living today remember being harshly and unjustly disciplined by parents who feared for our safety. In many black families parents often thought that they needed to "break the spirit" of a willful, creative child in order to prepare them for living in the world of racial apartheid. The brilliant writer Zora Neale Hurston grew up in a family where her mother and father disagreed about how the children should be raised. Her father feared that she would pay a price for her rebellious nature. She remembered him saying, "The white folks were not going to stand for it. I was going to be hung before I got grown." Taught to accept subordination, black children naturally felt in a state of psychological conflict. On one hand we had to possess enough self-esteem to seek education and self-advancement, yet on the other hand we had to know our place and stay in it. All too often parents used harsh discipline and punishment to teach black children their "proper place."

Prior to the civil rights movement, most parents felt it was a gesture of love to teach children skills that would enable them to survive in the existing culture of racial apartheid. At times this meant teaching habits of being that were not rooted in love. To break someone's spirit is not a gesture of love. It can and often does lead to what contemporary psychoanalysts have called "soul murder." Making it within a racist society often required and at times still requires both accommodation and assimilation. This often leads individual black people to develop a false self, one rooted in pretense and the denial of genuine feelings. The poet Paul Laurence Dunbar alluded to this false self when he wrote that "we wear the mask that grins and lies." All too often, though, the false self black folks donned to make it in the public white-dominated world was not easily shed when they reentered all-black private settings. The reliance on lies, subterfuge, and manipulation used to get by in the world outside the home often became the standard of behavior in the home. Importantly, many of the survival strategies black people learned which enabled them to cope with life in a racist culture were not positive skills when applied to intimate interpersonal relationships.

No lesson imprinted on the consciousness of most black people was as detrimental to black family life as the unequivocal belief that domination and subordination was a natural order, that the strong should rule over the weak and that the more powerful should rule over the powerless by any means necessary. Such thinking justified domestic violence. Men who believed, as most of them did, that women were the weaker sex, put on this earth to serve and obey the stronger sex, often used physical assault to subordinate their female partners. In his chapter "Enduring," Leon Litwack documents that domestic violence was common: "Much like their white counterparts, black males might lash out at women for no reason other than to exercise a male prerogative and to subdue independent spirits." Drawing on the life stories of well-known black figures such as Benjamin Mays, Zora Neale Hurston, and Louis Armstrong, who all witnessed their mothers and stepmothers being repeatedly beaten by the men in their lives, Litwack reports that there were many black couples who were able to sustain lasting marriages but not without "employing various strategies to balance the demands of labor and family."

Concern with material survival often precluded a focus on love in black families. Care and affection were often reserved for the very young. Toni Morrison offers a fictional account of a dialogue between mother and daughter in her novel *Sula* that reveals how notions of love differed among generations: "The second strange thing was Hannah's coming into her mother's room with an empty bowl and a peck of Kentucky Wonders and saying, 'Mama, did you ever love us?' " A silence follows these words, then the dialogue continues: "I mean, did you? You know. When we were little." The mother, Eva, responds initially by saying, "No. I don't reckon I did. Not the way you thinkin'." Enraged, Eva goes on: "You settin' here with your healthy-ass self and ax me did I love you?" Particularly annoyed by Hannah asking if she was ever playful with them, Eva proceeds to talk about struggling for survival: "No time. They wasn't no time. Not none. Soon as I got one day done here come a night. With you all coughin' and me watchin' so TB wouldn't take you off and if you was sleepin' quiet I thought, O Lord, they dead and put my hand over your mouth to feel if the breath was comin' what you talkin' 'bout did I love you girl I stayed alive for you can't you get that through your thick head . . ." Though fiction, the sentiments about love voiced in this passage echo the autobiographical comments Lorraine Hansberry made about her family when she described them as concerned only with material survival.

Masses of black people suffered extreme material lack before the civil rights struggle altered the nature of the job market. It makes perfect sense that generations of black folks learned to see caring for someone's material well-being as a primary gesture of love. Growing up in the fifties, I remember hearing grown-ups talk about relationships in terms of whether or not a man "provided" for the women and children in his life. Though our father was a stern, demanding, and punishing patriarch, when we were growing up Mama always praised him for providing for us. I can remember having a conversation with her in the early seventies about the nature of love like the fictional dialogue between Hannah and Eva Peace. A grown-up woman trying to understand "this thing called love," I was taking a critical look at my relationship with my father. I told Mama I did not feel Daddy loved me. And she told me, "Of course he loves you. He's taken care of all your needs all these years." Tears overwhelmed my words as I tried to explain to her that love was more than meeting someone's material needs—that it was about respect, care, knowledge, and responsibility. I was a graduate student then, reading philosophy and studying psychology. I knew there was more to loving than caring for material needs.

At the same time, I knew that working hard and sacrificing to meet material needs, to provide for one's family and kin, was a powerful gesture of care that could not be dismissed as having no value. Too many black children I knew did not have a father who worked hard and brought home the money that would be used not just for necessary food but for special treats. Our father worked hard to provide for seven children. Growing up as an only child with no father present, he had always had to work. His mother was stern and not very affectionate, yet they were deeply attached to each other. When she was dying, it was Mama who gave her tender loving care, washing her sick body, waiting on her hand and foot, and Daddy who provided. Providing really is not enough, even though it is crucial.

Without a doubt, in black life across classes we tend to place too much importance on material well-being, neglecting our emotional development. In his memoir *Colored People*, the famous black scholar Henry Louis Gates shares a revealing story about material longing. When he was growing up, his mother longed to buy a house. He recalls: "Mama came to believe early on that the key to wealth and comfort in America was owning property. She wanted a nice house for the same reason she liked nice things." As in so many other places in the United States, white people made it difficult, if not downright impossible, for black folks to buy property in Gates's hometown. When the sixties came, he and his father combined their financial resources and purchased the house owned by a white woman his mother had once worked for. Yet she was reluctant to move into the house. Explaining her reluctance, she stated: "Mrs. Thomas used to make me sit out in the kitchen, at a little wooden table, and eat the scraps. She was a mean woman. . . . She treated me bad. . . . The thought of moving into this house . . . I wanted to burn this house down." Here is a case where the pain of remembered trauma could not be assuaged by a material gift, no matter how longed for. Yet when we read the autobiographies and biographies of African-Americans we often hear similar stories. Stories where material status is offered as a balm to wounded spirits.

When we identify respect (coming from a root word meaning "to look at") as one of the dimensions of love, then it becomes clear that looking at ourselves and others means seeing the depths of who we are. Looking into the depths, we often come face-to-face with emotional trauma and woundedness. Throughout our history, African-Americans have poured energy into the struggle to achieve material well-being and status, in part to deny the impact of emotional woundedness. Truthfully, it is easier to acquire material comforts than to acquire love. When I interviewed the black rapper Ice Cube a few years ago and inquired how he coped with emotional pain, he responded by saying he "stuffs down the pain." Repression often turns pain into rage. For black men of all ages it is more acceptable to express rage than to give voice to emotional needs.

Talking recently with the popular young female rapper Lil' Kim, I asked about love in her life, and she responded: "Love. What's that? I have not known any love." Abandoned by parents who physically abused her, she had no way to understand love, but she did understand material survival by any means necessary. Her attitudes about love were cynical. Her focus in life was on attaining more money and fame. Listening to her, I realized that it is easier for a talented individual to move from rags to riches in our society than it is for them to know love. We use the satisfaction of material longing to deny the need to love and be loved.

Older black women entertainers, folks like Ella Baker and Etta James, reveal in their life stories how the search for love was often intermingled with the lust for fame and material luxury. It is no accident that the biography of Etta James is titled *Rage to Survive*. Emotionally abandoned by her mother at an early age, James found solace in her adopted kin. Dorothy, her mother, was a dashing, glamorous woman. James recalls: "I wanted to be part of Dorothy's taste and style, but I wasn't. I couldn't count on her. She never had a word of praise. Praise wasn't part of Dorothy's makeup she looked on me like a nuisance. Yet every time she 'round, my little heart would start to flutter." Raised by her adopted kin Mama Lu, Etta James was given love. Describing their relationship, she writes, "Mama Lu was strong in spirit but weak in body. She gave me all the loving encouragement I needed. She was my lifeline. . . . She was the only adult who tried to understand me. She was one of those older ladies who could put herself in the place of a little girl. I felt her compassion." When this loving mother figure died while Etta was still a girl, she once again suffered the trauma of abandonment.

Every black person knows individuals in the communities of their upbringing who were abandoned by biological mothers and fathers and raised by caring kin, usually by grandparents. Often caring kin do not give to their adopted children necessary emotional care, even though they provide shelter and meet material needs. Sustained loving care is needed to help heal the pain of emotional abandonment. Throughout our history in this nation, black people have tried to deny this pain—to act as though it does not affect our capacity to trust. Without trust there can be no genuine intimacy and love. Yet for those among us who have been abandoned, it is difficult, if not impossible, to trust. To move toward love, we must confront the pain of abandonment and loss. This means speaking what may have once been unspeakable.

So many black folks are grateful to the families and kin who raised them that it is difficult to be in any way critical of these environments. We know so well that often folks did the best that they could do given difficult and oftentimes harsh circumstances. However, to regain emotional well-being we have to be able to see the bad that emerged in these settings as well as the good. As long as black folks normalize loss and abandonment, acting as though it is an easy feat to overcome the psychological wounds this pain inflicts, we will not lay the necessary groundwork for emotional well-being that makes love possible.

*Three*

# the issue of self-love

RELIGIOUS TEACHINGS ABOUT love form the foundation of most black people's understanding of love's meaning. Even though we have diverse religious experiences, a vast majority of us still choose to identify as Christians. Listening to elders read the "good book" at home or listening to biblical scripture at church was for many of us the first place and at times the only place where the metaphysics of love was talked about. The two great commandments was that we love God and one another. As serious churchgoers, I and my peers were instructed to read and study all the books of the Bible. To this day I vividly recall the pleasure I felt reading what I had been "taught" was the love chapter. From the book of Corinthians I learned that to be loving meant to be kind, forgiving, and full of compassion. I learned that love was more important than faith or hope.

Yet the full vision of love evoked in the Scriptures was not realized in most of our homes. Writing about the link between Christian religious experience and love in his essay "The Mark of Churches," John Alexander reminds us that in theory the church is not only a place of love but a place where we learn to love. However, for Christians of all races these lessons often stay at the level of theory and never become practice. Alexander contends: "Instead, we keep paying far more attention to our work than to loving others. We spend more time cleaning our houses than caring for our relationships. We do whatever our 'thing' is and tend not to get around to love." When I was a child, I would often call attention to the failure of adults to live the beliefs they espoused in churches.

The tenderness and affection we associated with love as it was described in the Scriptures was primarily offered to young children and adult men. Growing up in the fifties, I was raised in a world where women endeavored to please their husbands, to be the angel in the house for the man who worked hard in the harsh world outside. In those days there were homes where fathers were absent, but there were no homes where there was not an adult male authority figure present. In all our homes, across classes, young children were allowed to express a wide range of emotions. As we grew older we were expected to develop a stiff upper lip, to not wear our heart on our sleeve. Wanting too much affection, either verbal or physical, was a sign of not growing up. Often we were taught that cultivating the ability to hide and mask emotions was central to the process of maturation.

To a grave extent, as black children moved from adolescence into adulthood we were expected to surrender attachment to all notions of love with the exception of romantic love. Much like the mother in Toni Morrison's *Sula,* the mothers in our community were concerned with making ends meet or acquiring the symbols of material success. Love was not always a central agenda. Like their white counterparts, black mothers of the fifties were trying to realize as much of the American dream as they could. The message they received was that it was their role as women to create a harmonious nuclear family. Television shows like *Leave It to Beaver, The Adventures of Ozzie & Harriet,* and *Father Knows Best* set the standard for what this family should be like. Our mothers watched these shows and so did we. There was no screaming, yelling, fights about money in these television families. Everything was in its place and everybody had a place. Often we measured our black families by these shows and found them wanting.

Our mothers, unlike their white counterparts, had to try and make a home in the midst of a racist world that had already sealed our fate, an unequal world waiting to tell us we were inferior, not smart enough, unworthy of love. Against this backdrop where blackness was not loved, our mothers had the task of making a home. As angels in the house they had to create a domestic world where resistance to racism was as much a part of the fabric of daily life as making beds and cooking meals. This was no easy task, since internalized racism meant we brought the values of white supremacy into our homes via the color caste system. Everyone knew that the lighter you were the luckier you were. And everyone judged you on the basis of your skin color.

In some homes, like the one I grew up in, mothers and fathers who had suffered pain because they were too dark rejected the values of the color caste system. Our brown-skinned mother, who had been raised by a mother who could pass for white, was determined that her children would not judge one another's value by skin color. When we were small she taught us to see the beauty in our diversity. Her seven children had differently colored skin and various hair textures, and each had its unique style and beauty. But Mama's wise parenting could not protect us from the world outside the home, which constantly reminded us that black was not the color to be, that the darker you were, the more you would suffer. Since we grew up in a world of racial apartheid, our sense of ourselves was shaped by blackness. Paradoxically in that black world we saw blackness revered and we saw it treated as the mark of shame. Importantly, we had a choice as to how to see it, and in our household we chose reverence.

Since racial segregation was the order of the day, we went to all-black schools and churches. Everyone we respected, all our authority figures were black. As children we did not know how limited their power was when it came to interacting with the dominant white world. Black families in the fifties, more than at any other time, endeavored to create a domestic life where racism did not overdetermine interaction, where childhood could be a time of innocence. Our father and mother did not talk about racism openly. Home was the sanctuary, the place were you could reinvent yourself no matter what you were forced to endure in the world outside the home. When our mother came home from working as a maid in the houses of well-off white women, she said very little about what happened there. Her joy was to be home with her family.

As children of the fifties, we learned our greatest lessons about race from segregated television. It was a constant reminder of our difference, of our subordinated status. In 1959, Douglas Sirk's melodrama *Imitation of Life* was the number four box-office hit. It provided the image of desirable womanhood. This film was an object lesson for females. Its message was clear. A good woman sacrifices everything for her family. As Susan Douglas points out in *Where the Girls Are: Growing Up Female with the Mass Media,* "Here we have Lana Turner as Laura, a selfish, blond bitch who is always primping in front of a mirror and is obsessed with her career. She is . . . the mother who once she gets a taste of professional success, callously relegates her child to the care of others so she can claw her way to the top. The word *sacrifice* means nothing to this bloodsucker." White and black girls knew we were not to imitate her. We were to be like Annie, the black maid, serving those we care about with endless love and affection and without complaint. Her daughter, Sarah Jane, tries to escape blackness by passing. Turning her back on blackness, Sarah Jane turns her back on Annie. She is of course punished. After the white world has used and rejected her, Sarah Jane comes back to blackness only to find that Annie has died of a broken heart. Douglas writes: "On her deathbed, with the violins and chorus of angelic soprano voices virtually pumping the water out of our tear ducts, Annie sets a new standard of female self-sacrifice." What appeared to the white viewer to be a new standard was already a common and long-standing tradition in black life. Annie leaves the bulk of her worldly goods to her wayward daughter, saying, "I want everything that's left to go to Sarah Jane . . . tell her I know I was selfish and if I loved her too much I was sorry."

To our young black eyes, it was Sarah Jane who embodied the new and troubling image. To black viewers, she symbolized a new rebellious generation who wanted access to the same opportunities their white counterparts desired, including a white partner. Her punishment was a warning to all of us; it was meant to keep us in our place. The film ends with an image of Sarah Jane running into the funeral and hurling herself on Annie's coffin, screaming, "Mama, I didn't mean it, I didn't mean it, can you hear me? I did love you, I did love you." This tragic figure represents the fate of uppity young black folks who step out of their place. Not only does Sarah Jane "kill" her mother by being rebellious, she loses out on the only love this culture is prepared to let her have.

Fathers are absent in *Imitation of Life*. The film revolves around issues which were seen as relevant primarily to women—service and self-sacrifice. It was pure propaganda. The image of a loving woman then was a woman who gives her life for those she cares about. But as the film makes clear, not all women make this choice. And even though many of our mothers worked hard to realize this ideal, as the recipients of this care we often saw how their sacrifices were unrewarded and unappreciated. Sacrificial mother love has been, and remains, a valued ideal in

THE ISSUE OF SELF-LOVE

black life. Contrary to the movie version, in real life mothers who sacrifice everything usually want something in return, whether it be obedience to their will, constant devotion, or something else. Many females who sacrifice everything are rageful and bitter. They may act out that rage in domineering and/or controlling behavior. More benignly striving to attain an idealized fantasy of mother love, some black mothers have actually hindered the self-development of their children by not teaching them how to be responsible for their lives. We now know that this is not a gesture of love.

When the contemporary feminist movement began, it helped many women to see that the sacrificial model was really designed by patriarchal men to keep women subordinated. It helped women distinguish between being a loving mother (which required the assertion of responsible selfhood and agency) and an anti-loving model which required that women repress all their own needs and desires to serve others. Some women were disturbed when feminist thinkers compelled everyone to acknowledge that the self-sacrificing woman was rarely genuinely loving, no matter how nurturing and caring her actions might appear. While these critiques have had an impact on younger women's construction of self and identity, overall they have not changed the idealization of the self-sacrificial woman in black life. She is still held to be the desired ideal.

SALVATION

Black women who embrace this ideal often have the
most tragic stories to tell of use, exploitation, and abandonment. Sadly, even though these revelations show that
this is an unhealthy and destructive way to be, this knowledge does not lead women to choose different habits of
being. Often women cling to this model because it is the
only available positive image, one that is constantly reinforced by mass media. The hit movie *Soul Food* was a
modern-day idealization and romanticization of the matriarchal mother. By not attending to her health needs, the
mother heroine dies an early and unnecessary death. Yet
the film makes her an icon. Most black folks know women
like this, but collectively black folks refuse to acknowledge
that selfless maternal giving is a sign of neither self-love
nor strength.

Often younger black females recognize this and refuse
to take on the mantle of martyr. Their awareness that the
self-sacrificing woman does not win the day is keen. They
know she does not receive love from anyone; gratitude
maybe, devotion sometimes, but love—rarely. Refusing to
be like Annie, the mother in *Imitation of Life*, they feel
there is more to gain by becoming like her daughter, Sarah
Jane—narcissistic, self-interested, and self-invested, out
for what they can get. Of course they are no more able to
love than the sacrificial caretaker. Since giving care is a
part of love, the sacrificial caretaker has some sense of

THE ISSUE OF SELF-LOVE

what loving entails, however incomplete. The callous, cynical, narcissistic female has no understanding of love.

Significantly, if black women are to choose love, we must rebel against both these models of desirable womanhood, the sacrificial martyr and the selfish diva. Nowadays hip-hop culture often idealizes the out-for-what-she-can-get, "what have you done for me lately" bitch goddess. But neither the opportunistic, greedy, self-involved diva nor the long-suffering maternal martyr represents self-loving womanhood. To choose love, we must choose a healthy model of female agency and self-actualization, one rooted in the understanding that when we love ourselves well (not in a selfish or narcissistic way), we are best able to love others. When we have healthy self-love, we know that individuals in our lives who demand of us self-destructive martyrdom do not care for our good, for our spiritual growth. Often men demand of black women that we assume a selfless caretaking role. In the popular film *The Best Man,* the black male "star" chooses a subordinated sacrificing partner over the independent self-actualized peer whom he really loves.

Most black males are not socialized to be caretakers, capable of nurturing their own or another's growth. Sexism has taught them to see loving, particularly nurturance and care, as a female task. When I interviewed black folks of all classes, about whether or not they were shown loving care by parents, the majority of respondents reported receiving loving care at some point from females but rarely from black males. Even those of us who were raised in two-parent nuclear-family homes described our fathers as emotionally distant and unavailable. Emotionally shut-down black males are often represented as epitomizing desirable masculinity.

The hard pose is deemed cool and alluring. Personified by rappers like the now-murdered Tupac Shakur, this pose has become the norm for most young black males between the ages of ten and twenty. Trying to live up to a code of hard masculine prowess usually leads black males who embrace this identity without question to devalue and destroy relationships. In his insightful book, *Finding Freedom: Writings from Death Row,* Jarvis Jay Masters addresses the myriad ways young black males don a mask of hardness to avoid acknowledging emotional vulnerability. To be vulnerable is to be weak. Jarvis tells the story of a fellow inmate who, knowing he was about to be attacked in the prison yard, calmly confronted his death as though this was the just and only possible outcome of his life. Fighting to the death, he could be seen as brave by his peers, for that is how it appeared on the surface. In actuality, he was without hope. In a letter he gave Jarvis to pass on to his daughter, this inmate shared: "Your Dad loves you. When you get this, my troubled life will have probably ended. But certainly not my love. . . . Please know how I've always held on to you, and have kept you always in my heart. . . . Please forgive me for all my wrongs. I wasn't a real father to you." Way too many black males know the experience of not being "real" fathers to the children they have sired yet failed to parent.

When I ask black males of all ages about the place of love in their lives, they express the desire to receive love but they do not talk about whether or not they know how to be loving. Young black males, like their female counterparts, will never know how to be "real" parents if they have known no loving care or have never learned from books or any other source what it means to be loving. Religious teachings were once the place where most of us learned ways to think deeply about love, but the place of those teachings has been usurped by mass media.

In general, the mass media tell us that black people are not loving, that our lives are so fraught with violence and aggression that we have no time to love. The most common image of a black person showing care in the mass media is the portrayal of the self-sacrificial black mother figure. When *The Cosby Show* first aired, many folks thought it was radical because it showed an upper-class black family. Although these images were new to television, all traditional black neighborhoods have been peopled by well-paid black professionals. One of the most unacknowledged realities in our lives is that racial integration is still quite a recent phenomenon. As late as the early seventies, the vast majority of materially privileged black people lived in all-black or predominately black neighborhoods. Racial integration led to black flight from areas that were once peopled by folks from diverse classes. Even though I was raised in a working-class home, I was always aware of the lifestyles of the black upper class in our community. It was only when racial integration allowed those individuals to move into more affluent nonblack communities that the black poor and working class ceased knowing intimately how their more privileged counterparts lived. In the days of total racial segregation, materially well-off black folks sent their children to the same schools and churches as those less privileged. The poor knew what the real lives of the privileged were like, and did not need to romanticize them.

After racial integration, with so many monied black folks leaving predominately black communities, a new generation of underprivileged children was born who often had no awareness of a black privileged class and how that class lived. It was these individuals who looked at *The Cosby Show* and believed it was based on pure fantasy. To them, the lifestyle depicted on the show was alien and therefore "not black," since they did not know any black folks who lived this way. In this sense their perceptions of blackness were as limited as the vision of racist whites who looked at *The Cosby Show* and believed it was pure fiction because they have never acknowledged the existence of black professionals—doctors, lawyers, et alia—or known anything about how they live. To this day a large majority of black doctors are educated at predominately black institutions. Most racist white folks know little about the existence of these institutions because they refuse to let go of their stereotypes about black lifestyle and educate themselves. They were eager to perpetuate the notion that the lifestyle portrayed on *The Cosby Show* was fantasy. It speaks to growing class divisions in black life that so many black folks also insisted that black family life as it was represented on *The Cosby Show* was not realistic.

While the upper-middle-class lifestyle depicted on this show was not representative, and could not be, since a majority of black people are poor and working class, the same holds true for shows that depict well-off white families as the norm. In her essay "In Memory of Darnel," Sylvia Metzler, a white woman, fondly recalls her friendship with a ten-year-old inner-city black boy who expressed surprise when he went to the suburbs and saw no trash and graffiti. He wanted to know, "How come black people's neighborhoods are so dirty and ugly?" She had the foresight to show him middle- and upper-class black neighborhoods as well as poor white neighborhoods so that the stereotypes he had received from representations in mass media, as well as those he had constructed from his limited knowledge, could be challenged.

Mass media tends to ignore the diversity of black experience. The worst aspects of black life are fictionalized on television and in cinema so as to reproduce race and class stereotypes. Before *The Cosby Show* challenged the narrow vision of blackness presented by television, the sitcom *Good Times* depicted a working-poor black nuclear family that constantly struggled to create a love ethic despite the hardships created by poverty and racism. More often than not, this show failed to radically challenge stereotypes. Instead it was the stereotypically "funny" behavior of the coonlike character J. J. that made the show a hit. His antics, not the efforts of the family to be loving, usually took center stage. *The Cosby Show* was a refreshing alternative because family life rooted in a love ethic was the central focus of the sitcom.

Critics often trash *The Cosby Show,* but despite its many flaws it remains one of the few mass-media productions that represents and celebrates a loving black family. We see very few mass-media images of loving black parents. Tragically, so many black families, like other families in our society, are unloving because continual lack of emotional and material resources makes living environments unnecessarily stressful. Instead of home being a place where love can grow, it becomes a breeding ground for despair, indifference, conflict, violence, and hate. Again, this is not to suggest by any means that materially privileged homes are necessarily loving ones; the point is simply that when people are not struggling to overcome depression caused by material lack and ongoing deprivation they have the psychic space to focus on loving if they choose. Still, one can choose to be loving no matter what one's economic status. When poor families are portrayed in mass media, they are always and only depicted as dysfunctional—spaces where love is absent and foolish behavior reigns supreme.

One of the major problems anyone faces when they endeavor to create affirming images of loving black people cross-class is the constant insistence that images of black life be realistic. In actuality the images of upper-class black lifestyles are as rooted in some aspects of reality as those of the poor and underclass; they are simply not representative. Most viewers confuse the two issues. Images of loving black people are often deemed unrealistic no matter the class of the characters portrayed. Even though a huge majority of destitute, poor, and working-class black folks may find it more difficult than their more privileged counterparts to create loving environments, material privilege does not ensure that one will be raised in a loving home. Loving black families exist cross-class. While they may not be the norm, everyone benefits when images of a loving family, whether real or fictional, are shown us. By focusing solely on situations of lovelessness in black life, whether fictive or real, the mass media participate in creating and sustaining environments of emotional deprivation in black life. Despite its flaws, *The Cosby Show*, and some of the predominately black sitcoms that followed in its wake, offered new and alternative images of black family life. Most importantly, family life was depicted as grounded in a love ethic.

Too much focus on "realistic" images has led the mass media to identify black experience solely with that which is most violently depraved, impoverished, and brutal. Yet these images are only one aspect of black life. Even if they constitute the norm in underclass neighborhoods, they do not represent the true reality of black experience, which is complex, multidimensional, and diverse. Why is an image of an uncaring out-for-what-she-can-get crack addict more "real" than the image of a churchgoing single mom who receives welfare and attends college courses in an effort to change her lot? Both images reflect realities I know—people I know. The fact is that racism, sexism, and class elitism together encourage individuals to assume that the negative image is more "real"; individuals approaching blackness from this biased perspective have an investment in presenting the negative image as the norm. To do so promotes, perpetuates, and sustains systems of domination based on class, race, and gender.

I can remember longing as a girl to see more images of black people on television. At that time I was not politically astute enough to ponder the issue of whether or not folks who embrace white supremacist thinking (as the vast majority of people in this culture do) would be either imaginatively qualified or at all interested in producing images of black people that would challenge stereotypes. When I grew up and became a cultural critic, it was clear to me that there was a basic contradiction here, that no one working from a white supremacist perspective would create positive decolonized images of black people. And that includes cultural producers who are white, black, or from other ethnic groups, as well as black people who have internalized racism. The vast majority of the images of black people we see in the mass media simply confirm and reinforce racist, sexist, and classist stereotypes. Now, we all know that stereotypes often exist in part because when any subordinate group is required by a dominant group to be a certain way in order to survive, the powerless group will take on those characteristics.

A white person who hires a black maid expecting that this person will be fat and funny just like Aunt Jemima on the pancake box will most likely find and choose that type of person. I can remember my amazement when first learning as an undergraduate that the image of the large mammy figure was largely a product of racist white imaginations. Historian Herbert Gutmann was one of the first scholars to call attention to the fact that research showed that the average black female who worked in a white home after slavery was usually a young underdeveloped girl and not the overweight mammy figure extolled by whites. This figure existed first in the white imagination and then the reality followed.

Wise decolonized black people have always known the power of representation. Early on this led many black actors eager to make it onstage and in television and movies to refuse to play certain roles. Lena Horne's father, in his role as a loving parent, met with white male studio executives to let them know that his daughter would not be playing a maid. It was not that these black folks believed working as a maid was not respectable work; they simply knew that the type of maid the racist white imagination would create for the screen would be stereotypically subordinate in ways that were not true to black women's real-life experiences.

Ironically, racial integration brought with it a greater demand for black representation. Black actors were suddenly urged by agents and publicists, many of them whites, to not look at roles from a moral or ethical perspective but to simply go for the experience and the money. In no time at all black actors were willing to depict characters that fulfilled every racist stereotype. This collusion with racist white folks has helped perpetuate racism; it has made it acceptable. One need only say that a dehumanizing image of blackness is true to real life in order to satisfy those who protest the constant reproduction of these images. Of course the bottom line is money. More recent films, like the much celebrated *Green Mile,* provide leading roles for black men who exist simply to serve the needs of unreconstructed, unenlightened whites. In this film a black male happily awaits execution for a crime he did not commit.

When it comes to the issue of love, the mass media basically represent black people as unloving. We may be portrayed as funny, angry, sexy, dashing, beautiful, sassy, and fierce, but we are rarely represented as loving. Despite her power as both a producer and a performer, Oprah Winfrey has for the most part failed to create radical new images of blackness. The emphasis is on the word *new*. Indeed, blackness is often mocked on her shows. Work she produces often shows black individuals caretaking and loving whites but rarely giving love to each other. This has become a norm on television and at the movies. When black characters are affectionate and caring, they are usually directing that care to white folks. This cannot surprise, given the ongoing reality of white supremacy. Indeed, the black servant white folks have treasured the most, from slavery to the present day, is the one who cared for them while neglecting himself or herself. This image is best evoked by Toni Morrison in her first novel, *The Bluest Eye*, when Miss Pauline rejects her own daughter Pecola, treating her family with contempt and rage, as she lavishes care and recognition on the white family for whom she works as a housekeeper. She chooses to "love" the little white girl while denying recognition and care to her own child.

Think about how many times we sit in a movie theater and watch hateful racist images of black people depicted on the screen. The vast majority of black people do not boycott or avoid such movies. They have become prime-time entertainment. These images do not teach love, they reinforce the message that blackness is hateful and unloving. When religious teachings formed the core of our understanding of love, all black people were admonished to love themselves and their neighbor as themselves. The new religion of mass media teaches just the opposite; it urges black people to accept the notion that we are always and only unloving, that even when we try to love we are derailed by lust. A perfect example of this is the film *The Best Man*. The films that show positive, sustained anti-patriarchal loving black families and heterosexual romance are rare and tend to fail at the box office, films like *Killer of Sheep, Sprung,* and more recently, *Woo.*

From Hollywood movies (*Harlem Nights, Jungle Fever, A Perfect World, The Pelican Brief, Waiting to Exhale, Soul*

*Food, Crooklyn, The Long Kiss Goodnight, Jackie Brown, A Time to Kill, Men in Black,* and *Independence Day,* to name a few) we learn that black folks will betray each other; that black men will give their lives to protect white folks while showing little or no concern for black family and friends; that black women are hostile castrating bitches who must be kept in check by any means necessary. These movies teach us that if we dare to love one another, our love will blossom but not last, that suffering, more than love, is our fate. Black folks may suffer together, joke, and have fun, but love will leave us. Importantly, what black characters do best on the television and movie screen is slaughter one another. Blackness represents violence and hate.

Until black people, and our allies in love and struggle, become militant about how we are represented on television, in movies, and in books, we will not see imaginative work that offers images of black characters who love. If love is not present in our imaginations, it will not be there in our lives.

A recent film targeted toward youth culture, *Slam,* depicts a progressive, loving relationship between a black male poet rapper and his Afro-Asian girlfriend. At a moment of crisis in the film the two characters argue, engaging in an amazingly constructive conflict that brings them closer together. They dialogue and communicate. This is a wonderful example of decolonized images. Rarely are black couples depicted processing—

communicating. This is progressive cinema. It entertains, challenges, and shows us new images.

That huge majority of black folks who identify as Christian or as believers in other religious faiths (Islam, Buddhism, Yoruba, and so on) need to return to sacred writings about love and embrace these as guides showing us the way to lead our lives. In biblical scriptures we are told that God "has set before us life and death." Our faith and our destiny as believers require that we choose love. That choice must be affirmed by changing how we regard ourselves and others, the images we choose to represent our world, the images we choose to endorse and value. Blackness cannot represent death when we choose life.

*Four*

# valuing ourselves rightly

N O ONE SPEAKS about the topic of black people and love without addressing issues of low self-esteem and self-hatred. It is by now common knowledge that the trauma of white supremacy and ongoing racist assault leaves deep psychic wounds. Whether the issue is a painful color caste system in black life or violent actions used by whites against blacks (denigrating speech, physical aggression, or dehumanizing representation), every day all black people encounter (as does everyone else) some expression of hatred toward blackness, whether we recognize it or not. Prone to recognize overt expressions of hating blackness, everyone tends to ignore constant covert expressions—a denigrating remark made by a seemingly friendly person, a stereotypically racist representation in a magazine or on a billboard. Or the myriad times in any given day when a white person takes public transportation and stands rather than sit next to a black person but sits if a seat opens up next to someone white. In predominately black environments someone may be casually using the word "nigger," or jokingly talking about black folks as lazy and not wanting to work. All these incidents are expressions of white supremacist thinking and action in daily life and the hatred of blackness that it condones and perpetuates.

"White supremacy" is a much more useful term than "racism" because it allows us both to hold nonblack folks accountable for acts of covert and overt racial aggression and to look at and challenge the ways black people internalize white supremacist thought and action. Tragically, most black folks first experience racist wounding in our own homes when our worth is judged at birth by the color of our skin or by the texture of our hair. Prior to militant movements for black power which challenged the denigration of black bodies using the in-your-face slogan "Black is beautiful," a large majority of black people simply accepted the notion of aesthetic inferiority in relation to whiteness. From the outset of our history in the United States, black folks aggressively challenged the notion that we were in any way intellectually inferior to white people. Consistently, black folks and our white allies in struggle called attention to black intellectual and artistic genius to resist racist stereotypes. White supremacist insistence that black people were lazy and unwilling to work hard was not internalized by black folks because their experiential knowledge countered this assumption; every day they saw black folks working from sunup to sundown, sometimes working themselves to death. Even in the face of racism's most vicious institution—slavery—initially on all fronts enslaved black folks refused to embrace white notions of our inferiority, but that changed when white racists doled out privileges and rewards on the basis of skin color. As this happened, it not only divided black folks from one another, creating a level of mistrust and suspicion that had not been there when all black folks were similar in skin color, it also laid the foundation for assimilation.

White supremacist practices of breeding through rape of black women by white masters produced mixed-race off-spring whose skin color and facial features were often radically different from the black norm. This led to the formation of a color caste aesthetic. While white racists had never deemed black people beautiful before, they had a higher aesthetic regard for racially mixed black folks. When that regard took the form of granting privileges and rewards on the basis of skin color, black people began to internalize similiar aesthetic values. To understand the color caste system and its impact on black life, we have to acknowledge the link between patriarchal abuse of black women's bodies and the overvaluation of fair skin. White supremacist formation of a color caste system where lighter skin was valued more than dark skin was the handiwork of white male patriarchs. Combining racist and sexist attitudes, individual white men showed favor toward the lighter-skinned breed of black folks that came into being as a result of their sexual assault of black women's bodies.

While white men used the bodies of darker-skinned black women as vessels to act out violent sexual lust without developing emotional bonds and ties, their biological ties to mixed-race black people led to the development of different and diverse sentiments. Whereas racist sexist iconography had deemed the darker-skinned black woman ugly and monstrous, a new standard of evaluation came into being to judge the value of fair-skinned females. Aesthetic eroticization of the lighter-skinned black female gave her higher status than that of darker females, creating a sordid context for competition and envy that extended far beyond slavery. How sad it must have been for enslaved black females to find themselves pitted against one another for small favors. Just as the dehumanization via objectification of enslaved black women's bodies was spearheaded by patriarchal white males, enslaved black males who embraced patriarchal thinking (no doubt the notion that women were inferior to men was already ingrained in their psyche before coming to the so-called New World, as women were subordinated to men in most archaic societies globally) began to value lighter-skinned women over their darker counterparts. Annals of history show that the lighter-skinned black male was often viewed with suspicion. He was seen as a threat to white male power. The lighter-skinned female was seen as more likely to affirm and uphold patriarchal white male power. As the object of white male desire, she was perceived as a creature the white male could subjugate at will.

As a strategy of colonization, encouraging enslaved blacks to embrace and uphold white supremacist aesthetics was a masterstroke. Teaching black folks to hate dark skin was one way to ensure that whether white oppressors were present or not, the values of white supremacy would still rule the day. Prominent patriarchal black male leaders who resisted racism on every other front showed a preference for light-skinned women. By their actions they made the color caste system acceptable. From slavery to the present day, dark-skinned children in black families risk not being as highly valued as lighter counterparts. In my lifetime the sixties black power movement was the only time that the color caste system was militantly challenged.

While the slogan "Black is beautiful" does not seem at all revolutionary today, before radical change in racial hierarchies it was taboo to publicly voice militant resistance to white supremacy by denouncing color caste. The sixties and early seventies were the time when black folks working in the mental-health field first began to directly speak about the way in which masses of black people had internalized racist assumptions about the ugliness of our bodies. The interventions created by the civil rights struggle and militant black resistance to white supremacy effectively raised consciousness and helped many black folks to divest themselves of white supremacist thinking. However, just as enslaved and newly freed black male leaders showed distinct preferences for fair skin, the leaders of our militant revolution did the same. They preached love of blackness even as they continued to give preferential treatment to those females who were lighter or in some cases white. In the sixties Malcolm X's decision to marry a darker-skinned sister, one chosen for him by his mentor and leader, Elijah Muhammad, was meant to set an example to other black men.

Undoubtedly male preference for fair-skinned partners led black mothers to feel that birthing fair-skinned children, especially if they were female, would heighten their chances of surviving and becoming a success. Heterosexual black males' lust for fair-skinned mates created a climate of hostile competition between black females of all skin colors. The negative impact of color caste systems has been most felt by children. Whether they are dark or fair, black children have been subjected to a level of shaming that is psychologically traumatic. Children degrade each other on the basis of skin color because they learn from adults that this is acceptable. Whether it be a light-skinned child lording it over a darker peer or a group of dark-skinned children mocking and ridiculing a fair-skinned peer, the intended outcome, to make that person ashamed of their physical features, is the same. It wounds the child's spirit, no matter their skin color.

Collectively, black folks already know what must change if we are to completely eradicate color caste systems. Many of those changes (the praising of diverse skin colors, the choice of variously hued black images in visual media, the refusal to equate dark skin with evil, and so on), which were put into place by militant civil rights struggles, were undermined by an unspoken backlash spearheaded by the white-dominated mass media. As we saw more images of black people on television and in movies, color caste overdetermined the nature of their roles. Dark-skinned people were usually cast in negative roles; they were the bad guys or the bad women—whores and prostitutes. The good people were always lighter. Black filmmaker Spike Lee brought national attention to the problem of color caste with his movie *School Daze,* but the movie simply reproduced this skin-color hierarchy; it did not challenge it or offer a new vision. More often than not, black-controlled mass media have been as invested in the color caste system as the dominant white culture. No matter the color of a filmmaker's skin, in movies and videos today dark-skinned black women are not likely to be cast in any role except that of demonic black bitch. In *Scary Movie,* a film made by black filmmakers, the black female character is depicted as hateful; ultimately she is brutally murdered by a group of white folks. Indeed, media fixation on mixed-race beauty has led to the institutionalization in the mass media of a color caste system similar to the one that reigned supreme in the Jim Crow years of racial apartheid.

Passive acceptance of internalized racism intensified with legal racial integration and the concomitant demand that black people who want to succeed "assimilate" the values and beliefs of the dominant white culture. As beloved black male leaders were assassinated, our militant movement to end white supremacy ended. Changes came (equal access to education, more and better job opportunities) and with them the assumption that black people no longer needed to engage in militant protest. By the end of the seventies black people were ready to sit back, relax, and live the American dream like everyone else. There was no longer an organized radical anti-racist movement to monitor whether or not all the changes were having a positive impact on black life.

On the one hand, one of the more serious changes, racial integration of public schools, gave black children equal access to the same levels of information offered white children who attended these institutions, but on the other hand, it meant we were now being taught for the most part by unenlightened white teachers with biased perspectives. Usually racist biases informed the knowledge black children received. And on a more concrete level the personal politics of white supremacy could be reenacted. The most rewarded black children were often those who were more docile and subordinate. The fairer they were, the more likely they were to be treated by teachers as capable of performing well.

In my segregated grade school and junior high school no black child was made to feel that allegiance to the race was determined by not liking to do one's work. If you played violin, studied French, or loved physics, no one could taunt you that these passions were expressing a desire to be white, as everyone was black, including our teachers. That changed with racial integration. In the predominately white high school one of my most attentive, caring white teachers also told me repeatedly that I would never have a black male partner because I was smart. There were no black males in the gifted classes in these schools. Their absence was not because they were not smart; it was indicative of the desire of white racists to keep black males away from contact with white females. Often black children were told at home that they needed to uplift the race by studying hard and proving their worth. Not wanting to worry and upset parents, black children of all classes usually did not share the various racist assaults they encountered in schools. Racial integration soon became a space where heightened levels of racial humiliation and shaming took place. Shame makes self-acceptance and self-love impossible.

Ironically, as more and more black people benefited economically from the changes brought about as a result of the civil rights struggle, the efforts to transform our culture in ways that would both eliminate white supremacist thinking and offer healing paradigms slackened. Most black thinkers acknowledge that internalized self-hatred is more pronounced now than it was when the economic circumstances of black people were far worse, when there was no social racial integration. Too late, progressive black people and our allies in struggle learned that legalized racial integration would not change white supremacist perspectives. Since anti-racist individuals did not control mass media, the media became the primary tool that would be used and is still used to convince black viewers, and everyone else, of black inferiority.

A pedagogy of racial hatred comes to us every day by way of the mass media. The images we see of black people are more often than not degrading and dehumanizing. Without an organized anti-racist political movement to vigilantly challenge media distortions, they rule the day. No one raises a fuss when the one black child in the television commercial is placed in a stereotypical role. No one urges mass boycott of films portraying black males as brutal rapists and murderers. No one acts as though the black actors who eagerly take roles that depict black people as being irrational, immoral, and lacking in basic intelligence are perpetuating white supremacy. Yet these images not only teach black folks and everyone else, especially young children who lack critical skills, that black people are hateful and unworthy of love, they teach white folks to fear black aggression. This fear allows white folks to feel justified when they treat black people in dehumanizing ways in daily life. A white woman who clutches her purse as she walks toward a young black male or female on the street sends the message not only that she fears for her safety but that she sees all black people as potential criminals.

We live in a society where we are daily confronting negative images of blackness. It takes courage and vigilance to create a context where self-love can emerge. When I recognized that black folks were collectively losing ground when it came to the practice of self-love, in a collection of essays, *Black Looks: Race and Representation*, I advocated that we renew anti-racist struggle in ways that would focus on loving blackness. In an essay titled "Loving Blackness as Political Resistance," I called attention to the reality that to end white supremacy we must create the conditions not only for black people to love blackness but for everyone else to love blackness. All black folks who love blackness recognize that it is not enough for us to be decolonized, that the non-black folks we work with, who teach our children, and so on, need consciousness raising that will enable them to see blackness differently. I concluded this essay by stating: "Collectively, black people and our allies in struggle are empowered when we practice self-love as a revolutionary intervention that undermines practices of domination. Loving blackness as political resistance transforms our ways of looking and being, and thus creates the conditions necessary for us to move against the forces of domination and death and reclaim black life." Loving blackness is more important than gaining access to material privilege. We know that many successful black people have assimilated white supremacist thinking and feel themselves and other black people to be unworthy, even though they may live and act as though they are the exception to the rule.

The issue of loving blackness goes beyond the question of race. Focus on racist assaults on black self-esteem has often caused us to ignore the impact of class. Even though we know that masses of black people are poor, we have often not linked the perpetuation of low self-esteem among non-privileged groups to the way all poor people are looked down upon in this society and treated accordingly. When an overwhelming majority of black people were poor because racial segregation denied us access to jobs and economic advancement, in our communities poverty was not a source of shame. Indeed, families often approached lack from a global perspective, relating their experience of material lack to that of folks in other countries. Since religion taught us that God loved the poor and the oppressed, we understood that to live simply, whether one had freely chosen that lot or not, was to live in harmony with divine will.

In the past, by not attaching negative stigmas to material lack, black people effectively refused to allow material status to determine substantive value. In our churches we were constantly taught that being rich was not a virtue, that it was more virtuous to love one's neighbor and to share resources, that greed was a sin. As the church started to become a site for class mobility (as churches evolved from places of worship to corporations, institutions requiring more money), these values were no longer emphasized. When this reality was coupled with a turning away from religious teachings as a practical guide for one's life, black folks of all classes began to buy into capitalist consumer thinking, which equated worth with material status and spread the message that "you are what you buy." The mass media, which had for the most part ignored the poor, showing us mostly the fictional lifestyles of the rich, began to tell everyone that to be poor was to be nothing.

More than racial assault, which black folks were quick to recognize and resist, this type of thinking was demoralizing. It was also terribly dangerous. It helped create a social climate in poor and destitute black communities where individuals were willing to rob, beat, and kill one another for material items. It helped lay the groundwork for the acceptance of a drug-based, capitalist, dog-eat-dog culture in poor communities where non-market values like sharing resources and neighborliness, which were once the norm, have been ridiculed, mocked, and all but erased. It also laid the groundwork for unprecedented levels of petty envy and hostility in communities where folks had once been bonded by respect for shared circumstances rooted in hardship.

Usually folks blame drugs for the moral breakdown in poor communities. But drugs, hard and soft, have always been present in black life. The social context in which they were once used was one that emphasized pleasure, not escape from dehumanization and pain. When poor and destitute people of any race are made to feel that they really have no right to exist because they lack the material goods that give life meaning, it is this immoral climate that sets the stage for widespread addiction. In recent years, when poverty has been depicted as a crime against humanity, poor people of all races have been seen as criminals and treated accordingly. This demoralization shames. It creates depression, despair, and the dangerous life-threatening nihilism black leaders talk about. It lays the emotional groundwork for widespread addiction.

Addiction is not about relatedness. Hence it destroys community. It creates a predatory culture, one where individuals regard each other with fear and loathing. In black families where addiction to drugs like heroin, cocaine, and crack prevail, bonds of affection and care are daily destroyed. Addiction knows no class. While materially privileged black people are able to deny and cover up the negative impact of substance abuse on their family life, emotional devastation is more readily visible in the lives of the poor and underclass. We know drug-addicted parents of all classes often neglect and abuse children, at times making them the object of profound, brutal rage. There are few places where this woundedness is attended to, where the post-traumatic stress individuals endure is addressed in a healing therapeutic environment.

Such environments would not solve the problem of poverty, but they would address the underlying issues of self-esteem and self-love. One can be poor and still be self-loving. A huge majority of successful black people who came from poor and/or working-class backgrounds know this truth. Just as material privilege will not ensure that any of us will be self-loving, poverty does not create low self-esteem and self-hatred. Until black people of all classes are willing to challenge negative attitudes toward the poor, greed will continue to be the force that ravishes all our diverse communities. Greed is sanctioned by those at the top of our class hierarchies and trickles down. The rich who condone exploitation, murder, and slavery in order to maintain their wealth are no different from the poor who prey on one another in order to satisfy material longings. Greed manufactures hate. Without challenging the politics of materialist greed we cannot create the climate in black life that will allow us to embrace non-market values.

From experience, black people know that no matter what our economic circumstance, we can create an environment that is permeated by a love ethic. Those of us who come from non-privileged backgrounds know this by heart because we felt the love in those places where material plenty was lacking. Love is especially available to us because it is a non-market value. We can create love wherever we are. Valuing ourselves rightly means we understand love to be the only foundation of being that will sustain us in both times of lack and times of plenty.

*Five*

# moving beyond shame

WHEN THE PHILOSOPHER Cornel West and I completed our book *Breaking Bread: Insurgent Black Intellectual Life*, we gave many lectures together. In these talks we often emphasized the importance of a love ethic. We talked about the importance of self-love. Again and again during question-and-answer periods, individuals in the audience would rise and ask us to say more about how we become self-loving. The practice of self-love is difficult for everyone in a society that is more concerned with profit than well-being, but it is even more difficult for black folks, as we must constantly resist the negative perceptions of blackness we are encouraged to embrace by the dominant culture.

Within the context of white supremacy, black people are often rewarded by racist white folks when we internalize racist thinking as a way of assimilating into the dominant culture. For example, a racially biased white employer who conveys stereotypical thinking about black folks to a prospective black employee will most likely select the person for the job who either agrees with his sentiments or does not challenge them. Throughout our history in this nation, every anti-racist struggle has stressed that decolonization is the only way black people can either unlearn or resist learning the racist biases taught everyone in this society beginning at birth. When a black child is newly born and those who stand around immediately evaluate the infant's value by his skin color, white supremacist thinking is taking place. The negative impact of the color caste system has already been discussed as a major impediment to healthy self-esteem among black people. Collectively decolonizing our minds means that every black person would learn to stop judging others on the basis of skin color.

Not all black people passively accept white supremacist thinking. However, it impacts on all our lives. We must be ever vigilant so that we do not end up evaluating each other using a standard of measurement created by white supremacist thinking. Often individual successful black people work in predominately white settings. In those environments we may often be treated by white folks as though we are special, different from the other black people whom they may perceive in stereotypical ways. Their behavior is aimed at breaking our sense of solidarity with other black people. When this happens individual black folks often internalize the notion that they are "superior" to most of their black peers. If such thinking prevails, they will often behave with the same racialized contempt that racist white individuals deploy. This is of course a strategy of re-subordination enacted to keep in place racial hierarchies that put white folks on top. Self-loving black people work to fend off attempts by white colleagues to pit them against other black people.

Decolonization is the necessary groundwork for the development of self-love. It offers us the tools to resist white supremacist thinking. The heart of decolonization is the recognition of equality among humans, coupled with the understanding that racial categories which negatively stigmatize blackness were created as a political tool of imperialist white domination. Most black people first confront white supremacy in the context of blackness, usually through discussion and/or responses to our appearance. Since the logic of white supremacy is that black is always bad and white always good, in order to decolonize, such thinking has to be rejected and replaced by the logic of self-acceptance. Learning to be positive, to affirm ourselves, is a way to cultivate self-love, to intervene on shaming that is racialized.

Significantly, during the worst periods of racial apartheid in the United States, black people were more acutely aware of the need to vigilantly resist internalizing white supremacist thought. Everything was segregated in the world I grew up in. Most white southerners expected black folks to behave in a manner indicating acceptance of subordination. In the presence of whites we were expected to not speak until we were spoken to, to never question anything a white person said, to always allow them preferential treatment, to obey them. The list could go on. Decolonized black people recognized not only that these expectations were unjust but that if we all conformed to them we would be both accepting and perpetuating the notion that it was our destiny to be second-class citizens. No black person could escape working within the constraints imposed on us by white supremacist capitalist patriarchy, but in all ways progressive decolonized black people found the means to resist.

Segregation meant that in our all black spaces, the institutions which governed our communities—church, school, social club—black folks could fully claim the subjectivity denied us by the larger white world. It was even possible for some clever individuals to live and prosper without really encountering the white power structure. As in the case of those escaped slaves (Maroons, renegades) who became insurgent resisters creating their own oppositional freedom culture in hidden locations, powerful individuals in our all-black communities were able to offer us liberatory ways to think about blackness. When we were growing up, my mother and father were careful to create an environment in our home where racial stereotypes were always challenged. My mother came from a family where her mother could pass for white and her father was very dark. Acutely sensitive to the conflicts color caste systems create, she was determined to raise her family in an environment where all would be regarded equally. This was important because our large family, like her family of origin, was made up of individuals with various shades and hues. Whenever anything appeared in the mass media that was negative and stereotypical about blackness, our mother would counter this information with constant affirmation of our worth and value as black people. I remember watching beauty pageants with Mama where all the contestants were white. She would say, "Look at them, they are nowhere near as beautiful or talented as you are." Or if she approved of a white female, she urged me to use this example to better myself.

Without knowing fancy political terms like "decolonization," our mother intuitively understood that consciously working to instill positive self-esteem in black children was an utter necessity. Her values were reinforced by all the black institutions in our community. Ironically, at that time everyone viewed the lack of black representation in mass media as a mark of racial injustice and white supremacist domination, but in retrospect our self-esteem as black people was stronger then than it is now because we were not constantly bombarded by dehumanizing images of ourselves. When we watched shows like *Tarzan* or *Amos 'n' Andy* that we enjoyed, we were ever aware that the images of blackness we saw on these programs were created by folks who, as Mama would say, "did not like us." Consequently, these images had to be viewed with a critical eye.

In my own family this critical vigilance began to change as the fruits of the civil rights struggle became more apparent. Mama's last child would watch television alone with no adult voices teaching her a resisting gaze. By the end of the sixties many black people felt they could sit back, relax, and exercise their full rights as citizens of this free nation. Once laws desegregated the country, new strategies had to be developed to keep black folks from equality, to keep black folks in place. While emerging as less racist than it had once been, television became the new vehicle for racist propaganda. Black people could be represented in negative ways, but those who had wanted there to be jobs for black actors could be appeased. Nothing pushed the lessons of a white supremacist aesthetic more than television, a medium where even dark-haired white women had to become blondes in order to succeed.

Since television has primarily exploited stereotypical images of blackness, small children held captive by these screen images from birth on absorb the message that black is inferior, unworthy, dumb, evil, and criminal. While well-meaning black parents attempt to counteract the racism of the culture by affirming blackness in their homes, their efforts are easily undermined by mass media. When black children are allowed to watch television unsupervised, white supremacist attitudes are taught them even before they reach grade school. It was easier for black folks to create positive images of ourselves when we were not daily bombarded by negative screen images. This may explain why individual black people came through the terrible period of racial apartheid with much better self-concepts than those of many young black people born when racial integration was more an accepted norm.

When there was no racial integration, black people were more vigilant about safeguarding the integrity of our lives in the midst of ongoing racist assault. Separate spaces also meant that racist biases in educational systems could be countered by wise black teachers. Those who attended all-black schools in the years before the militant black power struggle, institutions named for important black leaders

(Crispus Attucks, Booker T. Washington, George Washington Carver, et al.), were educated in a world where we were valued. While we studied the same lessons that were studied in the white schools, our teachers added lessons in black history and culture. Since everyone in the school system was black, we had perfect role models. No one doubted our ability to learn, to excel academically.

When our black schools were closed down and we were forced to integrate predominately white schools situated far away from our neighborhoods, it caused tremendous psychological depression. Regarded as first-class citizens in our beloved schools, we were now bussed to schools where we were treated as second-class citizens, where white teachers saw us as inferior, as savages, incapable of being their equals. When a black student excelled academically, they were regarded as the grand exception to the rule and treated by whites as a Negro pet. No psychologists or school counselors stood in the wings (nor do they stand there today) to help black children cope with the reality of moving from segregated schools where we had been valued to white schools where our teachers saw us only as a problem, where a great many of them actually hated us.

Few black people had foreseen that equal access to educational institutions would not have a positive impact if within those newly integrated classrooms black pupils would be taught by teachers perpetuating racist stereotypes, who encouraged us to feel shame and hatred for our race. Often the most well-meaning white teachers still held racist attitudes, which they expressed openly. When my well-meaning, supportive white female drama teacher told me no black man would ever love me because I was "too smart," she did not see herself as perpetuating a racist stereotype about black males. Once we left our all-black schools, gifted black male students "disappeared." They had always been visible in our all-black schools. At home our parents talked about this unfair treatment of black males; racist white folks simply did not want gifted white girls sitting next to black boys.

No one attended to the psychological needs of those boys who had once been recognized as gifted but were suddenly forced to go backward. One of the smartest black boys in my peer group had a breakdown shortly after graduation. Yet for the most part all these psychological traumas went unnoticed and the psychological pain they created went untreated. When we showed signs of psychological disturbance in our homes, fear of attending school when we had once loved our classes, we were encouraged to accept the pain as part of the civil rights struggle. Our mission was to endure the indignities inflicted upon us to uplift the race. Still, this did not, and does not, mean that we were not wounded by the process.

Placing our education in the hands of unenlightened

educators has always been dangerous and still is. Racist biases often shape both the information black students receive in schools and the manner in which they are treated when they seek empowerment by striving to excel academically. In their book *The Power of Soul,* Darlene and Derek Hopson tell this story: "When Derek was entering high school, he wanted to take college preparatory courses, yet despite his previously good grades, a white guidance counselor discouraged him from taking on such a challenge. Instead, the counselor advised Derek that he 'do something with his hands so he wouldn't be frustrated,' meaning that he pursue vocational or technical training rather than academics." As a loving advocate for her grandson, Derek's grandmother went to his school and intervened, helping him to forge ahead. African-American oral history is full of such narratives. Currently, many white teachers may be kind to black students and still direct them away from striving for academic excellence. This kindness often has led parental caregivers and students to let down their guard and not be as vigilant in detecting racial biases when they emerge from well-meaning souls.

A perfect example of misguided kindness happened recently when a young white Brooklyn schoolteacher, seemingly well-meaning, gave her predominately black schoolchildren the book *Nappy Hair* to read. When progressive black parents shared with her that they did not see this book as positive, she ignored their critique. When mainstream media focused on the incident, no one ever talked about the issue of why the black parents felt it was inappropriate reading. Instead, they were depicted as terrorizing this well-meaning teacher. While her image and her story were repeated on national television and in popular magazines, the parents who protested her choice of this text were never shown—their viewpoints never heard.

Though written by a well-educated black woman, the children's book *Nappy Hair* glorifies black self-hatred. While it accurately portrays the teasing about our hair many black females endure, it presents this negative signifying as positive. *Nappy Hair* tells the story of a dark-skinned black girl who is constantly ridiculed and mocked by everyone because of her hair. The book makes painful shaming seem like fun. The tone is humorous and witty. There is no critique of racialized shaming and no alternative images. After all the negative assaults on her appearance, humorously rendered, the little girl jumps for joy at the end of the book. In actuality black children who are shamed by someone mocking their appearance don't jump for joy. They are psychologically wounded.

At times the ways black children were and are wounded by racism intersect with other hurts inflicted by poverty, sexism, or other dysfunctional practices within the family. Children growing up in houses where substance abuse is the order of the day are always at risk. Throughout our history as black people in the United States, there has been so much emphasis on racism as a force undermining black family life that little attention is given to all the other factors that may impinge upon the development of positive self-esteem. Attending to the grievous injustices and injuries of racism need not lead black folks to ignore all the other issues that disturb the psyche. Shaming has been a central component of racial assault, yet it is also central to all other dehumanizing practices.

Within a culture of domination, shaming others is one way to assert coercive power and dominance. In traditional black folk culture some forms of humor promote forms of teasing that when used inappropriately become ways to humiliate and shame. For example, while there are positive dimensions to black expressive cultural practices like "signifying," there is often a thin line between humor that is funny, witty, and satirical, the intent of which is to entertain, and humor that is used as a weapon, to denigrate and shame. Children who are constantly shamed cannot build healthy self-esteem. And if this shaming continues into their young adulthood it often leads them to significant breakdowns in mental health.

In the anthology *Father Songs: Testimonies by African-American Sons and Daughters,* there are many stories about shaming. Brent Staples writes about his alcoholic father's habit of refusing at will to give money to his children, making them beg for it. At times they could turn the tables on him. Staples recalls: "When he didn't come through, the spot was heartbreakingly empty. The strategy then was to catch him in front of one of his brothers and shame him into it." Much cultural criticism, new and old, has been written about "playing the dozens." Underlying this game of humorously trading insults about one's mother (it is usually played by men) is the threat of shame. Often matriarchal mothers use shaming as a way of disciplining children. Who has not been in a public setting where diverse children are running around joyously expressing themselves while a lone black child sits obediently—silently? Everyone may comment about how well-behaved this child is. The fact that harsh authoritarian discipline may have produced this obedience is rarely noted. Usually when a black mother publicly uses harsh, emotionally abusive verbal assaults to discipline a child, folks are aghast, but that same verbal practice may have been utilized at home to create the "perfect" behavior so many folks admire in the silent, obedient child who responds only when addressed by an authority figure. Inappropriate criticism is usually a dynamic used to shame. All such practices undermine our capacity to create and/or sustain self-esteem.

Ironically and sadly in many black households where

parents are adamantly anti-racist, regimes of discipline and punishment exist that mirror those utilized by white supremacists to subordinate black people. Some of those practices are physical abuse, verbal aggression, shaming, and withholding of recognition (which may include refusal to give praise or show affection). Verbal assault is so common in American families of all races as to be considered simply normal. Whether it is has been normalized or not, we know that it has harmful consequences. In my book on black women and self-recovery, *Sisters of the Yam,* I talked about how much we show love by the way we communicate with one another, that we need to speak warmly and tenderly to one another. Mean-spirited, aggressive speech wounds. Lots of mothers responded positively to this section of the book, testifying that it is all too easy to forget that harsh words can wound and break the spirit.

It is often assumed that it is only poor women and men who verbally assault their children. These are usually the parents we see publicly yelling and ranting. But loud, aggressive speech is not the only harmful speech. In materially privileged homes children may be denigrated by parental caregivers who speak in calm monotones but nevertheless are expressing hurtful, damaging sentiments. Silence can also be used to humiliate and shame. An adult parent who refuses to acknowledge a child when spoken to conveys the message that the child is not worthy of attention. Many men use withdrawing into silence to express their power over others.

In Marlon Riggs's film *Tongues Untied,* a black male voices these sentiments: "Silence is our weapon. Silence is our shield." None of us can be self-loving if our presence is not recognized and valued.

Importantly, class plays no major role in determining whether or not we will be regarded by parents and care-givers as worthy. Many black folks from poor and work-ing-class backgrounds were given a foundation of love and recognition. This is crucial because many people choose to see poverty as the cause of child abuse whenever families are poor. There have always been loving families who lack material privilege. Children of all classes are abused. We need studies that document the strategies individuals use in homes lacking in material privilege to create care and respect in the midst of adversity. All too often the assump-tion prevails that one cannot expect poor people to be car-ing. We hear again and again that these individuals are too preoccupied to deal with their emotional development. Such thinking, coming initially from the ruling classes, has provided a convenient excuse that individuals who lack privilege can evoke to justify cruelty.

While it is true that as drug addiction becomes more commonplace in the homes of the poor it creates circum-stances that destroy care, still, substance abuse and its dysfunctions are the problem, not poverty. Since so many black families are poor and working class, it is more important for us to acknowledge and show how lacks in material privilege need not lead to emotional lacks. I know of no recent work that looks at how poor and working-class families create loving environments. White supremacist mainstream culture has always been and will always be primarily concerned with highlighting what does not work in black families. Progressive black people and our allies in struggle must do the work of calling attention to diverse strategies used to create positive self-esteem in all black families.

The heart of self-love is healthy self-esteem. In his insightful book *Six Pillars of Self-Esteem,* Nathaniel Branden defines these pillars as "the practice of living consciously; of self-acceptance; of self-responsibility; of self-assertiveness; of living purposefully; of personal integrity." Among these practices, personal integrity is one of the hardest, since it requires commitment to truth telling. Masking has been so central to black folks' survival within white supremacist culture that we have not always recognized the ways it harms self-esteem. Basically, masking invites us to create a false self, to misrepresent and dissimulate (that is, to take on whatever appearances are needed for a given situation). While masking was sometimes crucial to survival during the period of racial apartheid, those strategies destroy our capacity to be truth tellers when we adopt them in contemporary life. This cannot be stated often enough. Since patriarchal masculinity also encourages men to mask what they feel as a way of manipulating others, black males are especially at risk; they may be rewarded for being estranged from their feelings. Creating and maintaining personal integrity is especially hard in a culture of domination where lying is rewarded. Generally, in our nation citizens are lying more and more. When high-ranking political leaders lie and are rewarded it sends the message to all citizens that lying is the way to get ahead.

Often black folks striving to succeed may feel bombarded and conflicted when expectations from black peers and family differ from those of the predominately white world they work in. These individuals may construct a false self to get ahead in both these worlds. This produces inner conflict which undermines self-esteem. Importantly, the time has come for black people to courageously claim our right to personal integrity and refuse to don a false self for anyone. In the long run, individuals who self-betray by always masking and pretending suffer. Their mental and physical health is wrecked in the process. Shirley Chisholm remains one of the greatest black political leaders who always stood her ground when it came to the issue of personal integrity; that is why she titled her autobiography

*Unbought and Unbossed.* Politically, Dr. Joycelyn Elders had to cope with rejection for taking a courageous stand about sexuality, yet she has become a heroic example of personal integrity in a nation where individuals are willing to betray their beliefs to get ahead.

My mother's mother, Sarah Oldham, could not read or write. Yet she taught us all that we should be truth tellers, understanding that "our word is our bond." A hardworking woman, she would be seen by many as poor or indigent because she had no income beyond that received working on the land, yet she was rich in spirit. She and our grandfather Daddy Gus, her husband of more than seventy years, taught us the importance of living consciously, taking responsibility, and maintaining personal integrity. I emphasize this to state again that those who lack material privilege have as much access to spiritual and moral riches as anyone else. Currently, the poor are usually represented in mainstream culture as lacking in moral values, so we cannot state often enough that poverty is no indication of moral beliefs. Stigmatizing the poor in this way is one of the ways the collective self-esteem of poor people is continually assaulted in this society.

Since masses of black people are among the poor, our collective self-esteem is at risk whenever anyone tries to publicly insist that the poor are inherently inclined toward dishonesty and fraudulent behavior. Widespread addiction in our society manifests itself in the worst ways in poor communities because those who lack funds usually exploit others to pay for their substance abuse. Therapeutic work shows clearly that all substance abusers, irrespective of their class background, are likely to be dishonest. Addiction leads to lying. All addicts suffer a loss of self-esteem. Importantly, addiction must be effectively addressed in black communities to make way for a return to love.

Self-love is first expressed by the way we tend our bodies. We must work hard to love our black bodies in a white supremacist patriarchal culture. Loving our bodies does not mean simply liking the way we look. It means that we care for the well-being of those bodies by eating properly, exercising, and staying away from all addictions, including food. No mass media event has dramatized the extent to which food occupies a place of solace in black life as well as the recent movie *Soul Food*. Not only is the family matriarch suffering from diabetes, a disease no one need die from, she neglects her health caring for others. The movie shows this without making any meaningful critique. After her death the survivors do not change their diets, even though we saw the health problems and tragic consequences of bad diets. In *Feeding the Hungry Heart,* Geena Roth offers one of the most insightful accounts of the way we turn to food for solace, to give us the comfort we may lack in our emotional relationships. Much of the work on eating disorders in our culture focuses solely on the predicament of white females, so there is little published research on African-Americans and compulsive eating.

Many life-threatening ailments and diseases that afflict black people disproportionally to our numbers (diabetes, high blood pressure, heart disease, and kidney failure, to name just a few) can be avoided with sound preventive health care. This includes a healthy diet. Every African-American can express self-esteem first and foremost by caring for his or her body. And mental health is as crucial as physical well-being. Indeed, they are interrelated. Again and again I find black folks reluctant to seek mental-health care when they face emotional problems. Therapy is one available approach to healing. More and more individual black people are seeking help for emotional pain with professionals. This is a gesture of healthy self-esteem. Historically, therapy has been viewed suspiciously by black folks. Seeing therapy as suspect was rooted in the concrete reality that many mental-health-care practitioners held racist biases, especially white therapists. As greater racial awareness has entered therapeutic professions, more black folks choose therapy.

Emotional healing is a process that can take place in any setting where we are genuinely cared for, where problems and difficulties can be talked about and solutions found.

Folks without access to therapy can look to supportive friends, family members, and co-workers for help. When extreme racism could have made life unbearable for black folks, communities sustained themselves through a process like consciousness-raising. Talking together with one another about the impact of racism, black people created a shared community of concern and support. Everyone could be stronger in the face of adversity knowing they were not alone. When individuals experienced trauma from racist assault, they had support. Increasingly, individual black people feel they must confront the pain of racism alone.

Sadly, some black people have been made to feel ashamed of experiencing emotional pain in response to racial assault by a culture that increasingly suggests anyone who names their suffering is trying to use victim status to get over. This is definitely a tactic deployed by individuals who hope to sustain a regime of white supremacist domination. When black people, and other nonwhite groups, are told repeatedly that the problems they experience are their own fault, this de-legitimation not only censors and silences; it promotes insanity. Sane people with healthy self-esteem respond to oppression and exploitation by both acknowledging their pain and resisting. Although needed now, in the future it will be all the more necessary for black people and our allies in struggle to create a context for mental care that validates all the ways racist assault is traumatic while simultaneously creating programs for recovery.

There should be an entire body of work, both serious scholarship and popular material, focusing on black self-love. The absence of this literature is just another example of the way in which psychological trauma in the form of assaults on the self-esteem and souls of black folks is not taken seriously in our society. There should be books that do nothing but accentuate the positive, sharing theories and strategies of decolonization that enable self-love. Initially, when I began to seriously explore written material about the primacy of a love ethic in African-American life, I was astonished that there was so little information. We need more. It's as simple as that. Without an organized, mass-based, progressive, anti-racist political movement, which we also need, it is all the more crucial that our homes become sites of resistance, where we create the oppositional spaces where we can be self-loving. These are the spaces where we have power. We can make homeplace the site where love that is the foundation of all healthy self-esteem exists.

*Six*

# mama love

AN OVERWHELMING MAJORITY of black folks will testify that they were first loved by a black woman. In African-American life black women have been love's practitioners. Amazingly, despite how easy it would have been or would be for black women to give up on love given the adversity we have had to confront on these shores, many of us have held to our hope in love because we believe in love's power to heal and renew, to reconcile and transform. It has not been easy for black women to maintain faith in love in a society that has systematically devalued our bodies and our beings. When we look back at the history of black women, from slavery to the present day, we see ourselves represented first and foremost as inferior beasts of burden, compelled by circumstance to serve the needs of others.

In *Darkwater: Voices from Within the Veil,* published in 1920, W. E. B. Du Bois published the essay "Damnation of Women" as an homage to enslaved black women and their daughters. He writes: "The crushing weight of slavery fell on black women. Under it there was no legal marriage, no legal family, no legal control over children. . . . Out of this what sort of black women can be born into the world of today? There are those who hasten to answer this query in scathing terms and who say lightly and repeatedly that out of black slavery came nothing decent in womanhood; that adultery and uncleanliness were their heritage and are their continued portion." Du Bois wrote his essay to defend black women. While he praised black female leaders from slavery on, he urged that black people support "the uplifting of women" by challenging sexism and gender discrimination, but his advice was not heeded.

Rape of black women during slavery distinguished our experience from that of black men, whose harsh lot as workers we shared. Violated black females had to cope with the disgust and disdain of everyone around them. No one cared about the impact of traumatic rape on their psyches. Enslaved black women were caught in a paradoxical situation. When they coped with rape at the hands of

white and black men with grace, they were seen by their
oppressors as superhuman, animalistic and monstrous,
capable of enduring atrocities that would break the spirits
of "real women." As black women testified in slave narratives, even other black people held them responsible for
circumstances over which they had no control. No one
praised black women's generosity of heart, their willingness to practice forgiveness.

Often enslaved black women found strength to love
through religious belief. Sojourner Truth felt that she had
been called to become an anti-racist activist. Her vision
and courage were rooted in a sense of divine calling. As
with many black women who preceded her, prayer was the
connection between her and divine spirit. Prayer along
with religious beliefs allowed enslaved black females to
develop an oppositional spirit where they were able to
resist seeing themselves through the eyes of their oppressors. They saw themselves as God's children with a right to
freedom and justice. In *The Narrative of Sojourner Truth*,
edited by Margaret Washington, she is described as utterly
devoted to the will of divine spirit: "No doubt, no hesita-
tion, no despondency, spreads a cloud over her soul; but
all is bright, clear, positive, and at times ecstatic. Her trust
is in God and from him she looks for good, and not evil.
She feels that 'perfect love casteth out fear.' " Loving God

not only helped black women survive, sacred teachings about love provided a metaphysics that guided and shaped human interaction.

Just as some enslaved black women survived by opening their hearts and trusting in divine will, other black women survived by hardening their hearts, by shutting down their emotions. Like contemporary trauma victims who disassociate as a means of enduring and surviving brutal assaults, some enslaved black women just cut off feelings. In *Trauma and Recovery,* Judith Herman highlights the aftermath of violence on the psyche, emphasizing the toll on victims: "Traumatized people feel utterly abandoned, utterly alone, cast out of the human and divine systems of care and protection that sustain life. Thereafter, a sense of alienation, of disconnection, pervades every relationship, from the most intimate familial bonds to the most abstract affiliations of community and religion. When trust is lost, traumatized people feel that they belong more to the dead than to the living." Once slavery was abolished, there were no scholars ready to interview the slaves about post-traumatic stress disorder. Few documents recorded anything about the emotional well-being of the newly freed slaves. All the emphasis was on material survival.

During slavery, enslaved black people never behaved as though material comforts were all that mattered in life.

Historical material documents how hard folks worked to establish and maintain emotional ties with one another. The desire to respect ties between biological family members was so intense that newly freed slaves often spent lifetimes searching for their kin. Enslaved Africans made beautiful art, created music that still dazzles the world, and sought to find spaces, however relative, of self-actualization and self-development despite bondage. Religion became the location where creativity of mind and heart could freely be given expression. In worship the slaves could know joy and delight, could know experientially that they were more than their pain.

The incredible resiliency of spirit enslaved black people possessed has often deflected attention away from the legacy of psychological woundedness the experiences of enslavement generated. In the past, black leaders were so eager to insist that black folks had triumphed over the evils of slavery and the brutality of racial apartheid that there was little cultural space to talk psychoanalytically about post-traumatic stress and negative scars on the psyche. While historical documents provide evidence proving that newly freed slaves often set up households based on the same principles of coercive domination that they had experienced, these facts have not led to enough discussion about the black experience of trauma and recovery. It has taken almost a century for people to feel free to talk about a continuum of psychological woundedness that still impacts our collective mental health in black life.

This reality is nowhere more evident than in the lives of African-American women, as it was during slavery that we were first represented as licentious, lustful, untrustworthy betrayers. These racist and sexist stereotypes were first articulated by powerful white men eager to explain away their use and abuse of the black female body they claimed to hate so much. In a world rooted in patriarchal religious teachings it was much shrewder for all white folks to blame black women for abuse by claiming they were monstrous sexual temptresses who lured good upright white men into sin. By accepting this scenario, white women did not have to acknowledge their connections to white male terrorists and rapists. Since sexual slavery (i.e., women bound to men in conditions of lifelong servitude and subordination) continued even as slavery based on race ended, black women still had to face a culture that perceived and still perceives us as the embodiment of these stereotypes. To make matters worse, black men and pious black women often internalized many sexist/racist ways of seeing black females. All these factors together sustain a psychological climate that is conducive to the formation of self-hate rather than self-love.

Living in a culture that constantly devalues us, black

women must work doubly hard to be loving. Coping with the stigma of being labeled whores and prostitutes, licentious and lewd, led black women in the early twentieth century to place undue emphasis on puritanical virtue. Believing that claiming the status of virtuous womanhood would automatically dispel negative stereotypes, black females often surrendered emotional playfulness and sensuality in favor of a stern maternal stance. This created the same tense divisions between black women that variations in their color created, for all black women were subject to being seen as either madonnas or whores. Both representations required that black females surrender a complex emotional universe and conform to a stereotype. Since a hatred of the female body and its natural functions was at the root of both stereotypes, no matter the identity a black female embraced, madonna or whore, it was unlikely she would learn to love her physicality.

One of the most important contributions that came from a fusion of the sixties' black power struggle, sexual liberation, and feminist movement was the emphasis on accepting and loving the body. Ideas from these three movements helped release black women and all women from the tryanny of patriarchal woman-hating. Linking the notion that black is beautiful with a vision of female entitlement to sexual pleasure meant that all black women no longer had to fear being judged as without virtue if we were sexual. Black female self-love could be fully realized only when individuals no longer internalized negative stereotypes. Black women who had carried a burden of shame in the mid-1900s and after because they had babies without being married or had to marry because they were pregnant no longer had to suffer disdainful attacks from all sides. The attacks continued, but the way an individual woman coped with being attacked was changed forever.

New and better birth control also enabled more black women to enter the seventies asserting positive sexual agency, including ensuring that we were not the victims of unwanted pregnancies. Unlike many of my white female college mates and peers, I and other black women I knew did not use abortion as a means of birth control. We were obsessed with using appropriate contraception so that we would not need abortions. At this time Shirley Chisholm was among the first feminist woman to speak out against unwanted pregnancy. She urged black people to support contraception and abortion when needed. With amazing courage she called attention to the large numbers of black women who lost their lives seeking unsafe abortions.

Chisholm's work was never given the attention it rightfully deserved largely because she uncovered data that countered racist and sexist stereotypes which suggested that poor black women (and for that matter black females of all classes) were eager to give birth so they could receive welfare. Her work and that of other feminist women showed that most mature women when given options did not want to bring an unwanted pregnancy to term. Patriarchal male leaders in the black church, with the help of puritanical, punishing matriarchs, intervened on progressive reproductive-rights efforts by encouraging black females to believe they would be punished by God if they had abortions. Conservatives, black and white, denounce welfare even though they made, and make, it difficult for poor black females to receive needed sex education and necessary abortions. If all black communities took a more progressive stance on sexuality and reproductive rights, then there would be fewer unwanted pregnancies.

Despite changes in the ways the larger culture thinks about sexuality, many young black females still risk pregnancy because they are responding to the desires of males, usually older, who want not only to be sexual with them but to do so without using condoms or other birth-control devices. To not put herself at risk, a young female has to possess healthy self-esteem that makes it possible for her to not only say no but to engage as well in the preventive health care that keeps her from placing herself in any situation where she might be in jeopardy. There is little work done on the prevalence of date rape in black communities. Yet daily young females are coerced sexually by men. Of course, when coercion is taking place, there is no use of a contraceptive device. Revealing tell-all accounts of his own and other black males' rapes of unsuspecting females in the memoir *Makes Me Wanna Holler: A Young Black Man in America,* Nathan McCall tells how his teenage son asked him, "Is it all right to take it from a girl if you take her out and she won't give it up?" The fact that black females are perceived as a group that men can rape without consequences is part of that continuum of devaluing black female bodies that began during slavery.

Charlotte Pierce-Baker has edited a groundbreaking collection of black women's stories of rape, *Surviving the Silence,* which reminds readers of the extent to which this society has never taken the rape of black women seriously. Knowing this, black females who are raped often say nothing and live with the troubling psychic aftermath of this trauma. Nothing is more heartbreaking in these stories than the lack of support for their recovery. Time and time again, a black female elder blames the victim or demands silence to protect the perpetrator. These were the lessons many black folks learned in the context of slavery: protect evil rather than correct it. Some black women learned these lessons as well and turn their backs on female victims of male brutality.

Developing positive self-esteem about our bodies and beings continues to be arduous for black females in a society that consistently represents us negatively. Promoting devaluation and hatred of black females has been absolutely politically strategic within white supremacist capitalist patriarchy. As long as folks hate and fear black women, seeing us as sluts and prostitutes, there is little chance that masses of white men will ever choose to marry black women. As long as black females are hated and despised, the purity of white families remains intact. Ironically, while contemporary movies like *The Bodyguard, Rich Man's Wife,* and *Bulworth* exploit the taboo by portraying love relationships between black women and white men, in the end these bondings are always disastrous. The black female is stereotypically represented as overly sexual, desired only for her body. And in the one film where the black female is married to the rich white male, she is portrayed as an ex–drug addict/user/ho/betrayer. White supremacist thinking keeps these racist/sexist stereotypes alive in everyone's imagination for a reason; it both encourages and allows for white male lust for black females even as it encourages this lust to stay on the level of objectification and degradation.

Often when black women are romantically approached by white men in real life, the black female does not respond affirmatively because she fears that he may project racist/sexist fantasies onto her. No one talks about white men loving black women. Such unions are always represented as being always and only about sexual lust. This will not change until more anti-racist people, especially white males, share their love stories and offer a different picture.

Images of black women in movies by black filmmakers, mostly males, have done little to change racist/sexist stereotypes. Spike Lee, John Singleton, and a host of other black male artists continue to project sexist images of black womanhood. In their films, when the black female is not a sex object she is often depicted as a treacherous, evil bitch. Since most black males share with white males patriarchal thinking that already depicts females as innately evil and lustful, they have not offered the world alternative ways to think about black women. Instead, way too many sexist black males have exploited black females with the same indifference and lack of connection that characterized white male use and abuse of black females during slavery. Since these men, like their white counterparts, see females as subordinates, they see nothing wrong with their attitudes.

The most troubling aspect of Nathan McCall's confessions of his abuse and rape of black females is the lack of critical interrogation of his motives and the failure to indicate how his attitudes changed. When his son wants to know if it's acceptable to date-rape, he can only tell him to imagine a guy wanting to do the same thing to his mother. McCall never shows that he has unlearned sexist thinking. It is difficult to imagine that had he been callously describing the senseless rape and violation of white females without ever showing deep critical reflection or remorse, his book would be a bestseller. Given racism and sexism, his use and abuse of black women is merely the colorful backdrop that gives him street credentials and makes him more interesting. He never talks about learning the meaning of love, or of loving black females. His story is not uncommon. Cultural critic, activist, and writer Kevin Powell is one young black male who has outspokenly criticized sexism and violence against women. Significantly, he began his public discussion of woman-hating by offering personal confessions. In the autobiographical work *Keepin' It Real: Post-MTV Reflections on Race, Sex, and Politics*, Powell scrutinizes his relationship with all the women in his life. His journey, always honest and often painful, begins with the tumultuous but pivotal relationship with his mother. It was that relationship, filled with love, resentment, anger, and fear, that Powell sought to re-create or, at other times, obliterate in his intimate relationships with women later in life.

Until black females are no longer collectively perceived always and only through racist and sexist stereotypes, cultivating self-love will remain a difficult, though by no means impossible, task. Throwing off the burden placed on us by sexism and racism is one of the ways that we love ourselves and other black women. All loving black females threaten the status quo. Clearly, the most troubled black females are those who try to find a place for themselves within the existing paradigms by internalizing self-hatred. When any black female acts out in a manner that is in keeping with negative stereotypes, there is more room for her in the existing social structure than there is for decolonized black women who challenge the status quo. No doubt this is why so many young black women feel that the only options they have are to claim the roles of bitch and ho. By embracing these labels they can feel a false sense of agency. They fit within the dominant culture's idea of them.

Like their enslaved counterparts, these black females find the strength to survive through processes of disconnection and disassociation. They feel that being emotionally open and vulnerable, which we must all be if we are to love and be loved, only means that they will be wounded or, worse, crushed. Better not to have a heart than to have one that is constantly breaking. When I first began to teach women's studies courses focusing on black women, students often described their perceptions of adult black women using words like "stern," "strong," and "hard." Again and again I would hear students of all colors describe black women they saw on the streets as unsmiling and rigid. When we would later examine the details of black women's lives, facts that document the reality that many of us live in poverty, or do low-paying jobs without access to health care; that we are likely to be single for much of our adult life; that of the three leading causes of death for women, heart disease, breast cancer, and lung cancer, we are disporportionately at risk and more likely to die if we have these illnesses; and that we are daily the victims of unacknowledged verbal and physical assault both in the streets and in our homes, they understood the reasons black females do not appear open and playful. After examining these facts students would often say, "What do black women have to smile about?"

Since adversity has been so unrelenting in black women's lives, a great many black females are losing faith. When I meet with young black girls who are already deeply cynical about their fate in this society, I am reminded of the reality that hatred of black womanhood is ever present in this culture and gathering added momentum. The young feel its painful assaults before they have established a sense of self strong enough to ward off this threat. Again and again I am reminded of the fact that as racial integration removed barriers that once forbade contact and connection, invisible, unspoken barriers were put up in their place. In my adult life I rarely hear a white person express his contempt and disdain for black womanhood, but I see it in the images white people create. I see it in the way young white women treat black women they have hired as nannies; at times their interaction is like a scene from the antebellum South. No wonder then that black girls can sit and tell me that no one sees them as desirable, especially if they have dark skin. Girls growing up in segregated black communities and schools did not doubt their value as profoundly as girls did in integrated environments. In segregated spaces black people controlled representations yet we did project images of ourselves that were constantly self-hating and ugly. For black girls to have a chance to build healthy self-esteem in an integrated colonizing environment, there must be oppositional strategies and places that promote decolonization.

Weary adult black women often abandon the emotional care of young females. In the face of unchanged racist and sexist stereotypes, older black women often harden their hearts so as not to feel the pain. Numb emotionally, they are often aggressively judgmental and punishing in their attitudes toward younger females. Any black woman who reads contemporary fiction by African-American women finds there narrative after narrative of mothers emotionally shaming and wounding their daughters. As a girl I was always disturbed when hearing the old saying "Black women raise their daughters and love their sons." It suggested not only that girls did not matter but that the only role our mothers played in relationship to us was to keep us in check, to discipline and punish us or teach us how to conform to a woman's lot, showing us how to be subordinate and servile. Often when a young black female has been hurt, attacked, raped, or incested, she is blamed by stern black matriarchs. I have witnessed daughters telling their mothers about sexual abuse. These mothers respond with harsh, interrogating questions denying the truth of their daughters' words rather than giving sympathy or offering therapeutic care. These acts of unlove are what lead so many black females to harden their hearts as they strive to make the transition from being teenagers to young adulthood. They lose faith. This loss can be as detrimental to the psyche as addictions. Confirming this in her book *Stop Being Mean to Yourself,* Melody Beattie contends: "There are many drugs that can injure the body and deaden the soul—cocaine, alcohol, heroin, marijuana. But there are other drugs whose narcotic power we overlook. Disillusionment and betrayal can grind away at our souls until all our faith and hope are gone. The cumulative effect of a lifetime of disappointments can leave us wandering around confused, lost, and dulled. Whether it happens in one moment or over many years, losing faith deadens the spirit." Popular racist and sexist myths that depict black women as strong matriarchs able to endure any and all blows to the spirit keep everyone from acknowledging black female heartache and woundedness. To avoid pain, black females often turn to substance abuse or to psychic self-mutilation by disconnecting and closing the door to their hearts.

Women who harden their hearts, who turn away from love, are unforgiving in their relationships with other females. This is as true of black women as it is of any group of women in this society. In my book about writing, *Remembered Rapture,* I included an essay discussing the fact that black women who write about my work have done so with a level of mean-spirited hatefulness that is awesomely intense. Audre Lorde was one of the first black female feminist thinkers to call attention to the rage and hostility black women unleash on one another. In her insightful essay "Eye to Eye," Lorde wrote, "Why do Black women reserve a particular voice of fury and disappointment for each other? Who is it we must destroy when we attack each other with that tone of predetermined and correct annihilation? . . . This cruelty between us, this harshness, is a piece of the legacy of hate with which we were inoculated." Ironically, when a black woman reaches out with tenderness and care, other black females may see her as not tough enough, as not a "real black woman," a projection that once again denies us our full humanity.

Lorde was clear about the fact that many black women had to unlearn their own sexist woman-hating to love themselves and other black women. She confesses, "Until now, there has been little that taught us how to be kind to each other. To the rest of the world, yes, but not to our-selves. There have been few external examples of how to treat another Black woman with kindness, deference, ten-derness or an appreciative smile." When I first read this essay it seemed alien to my experience. And I was struck by the fact that Lorde was writing from her experience growing up in the urban North, the child of West Indian parents. In the southern world of my upbringing much of the sweetness of life came from the tenderness of black women. Significantly, these women were often poor and working class. There was not the level of competition between them that characterized middle- and upper-class black women.

I was raised in a two-parent household with five sisters and one brother, and my mother consciously talked with her girls about the ways competition and envy divide and separate. She let us know in no uncertain terms that there would be no catfights, no wars over boys, that we would respect and love one another as sisters. Her powerful les-sons in sisterhood have stayed with us. We know how to love one another. We know how to open our hearts. Black women make a mistake when we assume that closing our selves off and wearing the mask of indifference makes us strong or keeps us well. Repressing our feelings leads to stress and that leads to a variety of illnesses. Allowing our-selves to feel only rage is equally debilitating. To love ourselves rightly, to love others, we have to claim all our emotions.

Following in the path of Sojourner Truth and other wise black women elders, black females must constantly assert our full humanity to counter the impact of dehumanizing forces. Expressing our full range of emotions is healing to the spirit and engages us in the practice of self-acceptance, which is so essential to self-love. Underneath the stern expression I saw my mother and many of her friends wear was an ongoing fear that if they let their guards down, even for a minute, they would be disrespected, hurt, or violated in some way. To love, we have to let fear go and live faith-based lives. Living in faith means that we recognize, as our wise black female ancestors did, that we do have the power to decolonize our minds, invent ourselves, and dwell in the spirit of love that is our true destiny.

*Seven*

# cherishing single mothers

THROUGHOUT THE UNITED States there are more single-parent households than ever before in the nation's history. Yet black women remain the one group of single parents who are consistently attacked. Assailed on all sides by a white supremacist culture that stereotypes black females as "welfare queens," by black men who claim they are the victims of these castrating breeders who would rather live off welfare than have a good man support them, and by the shaming judgment of a nation that castigates unmarried poor women who birth children, while idolizing unmarried rich and famous women who choose to parent, single black mothers are increasingly represented in the mass media as harsh, uncaring parents.

A large group of black single mothers parent alone because they are divorced. They are working mothers. Like their nonblack counterparts who receive state aid, most of them would relish being economically supported by a caring male provider. It's a myth that black women prefer to raise children alone. Even most single professional women living alone who choose to adopt a child would prefer sharing parenting with a caring partner. Parenting alone is difficult work. No one knows this better than black women. And it is even more difficult when women are poor.

Barbara Omolade's *The Rising Song of African-American Women* includes one of the most insightful discussions about black single mothers ever written, in a chapter titled "It's a Family Affair." Throughout this essay she draws together facts and figures to counter negative stereotypes about black single mothers. Omolade writes: "Most black single mothers are the working poor. We do domestic work, sew in factories, and are self-employed as merchants and caterers. We commute daily to city, state, and federal government agencies. As paralegals, aides, and clerks, we are the backbone of the hospital, child care, and nursing home systems. Although the wages are low and the work tedious, black women stay with city jobs for years because they offer stability and benefits." More often than not, when the topic is black single mothers, the image evoked is one of black women on welfare. Working black single mothers tend to be ignored in this society unless they can be evoked as a means of pathologizing black family life.

For a long time working black single mothers were simply ignored. When the white supremacist, patriarchal mass media wanted to paint a portrait of pathology, it highlighted black women receiving welfare. Usually the spotlight would focus on an individual black woman with four or more children by different men who was lying to the system to receive more aid. It has never mattered to the listening public that this image is not representative. However, in recent years, as more concrete statistics about who actually receives aid and how much money recipients are actually given are made public, anyone who is not blinded by biases has to face the extent to which negative images of black women on welfare are flaunted as a way to scapegoat them and leave unquestioned issues of class, race, and imperialism when it comes to the allocation of funding.

I want to place a spotlight on black single mothers to talk about the concrete practice of a love ethic in black life because there is so much evidence to document that this group, more than any other, against the odds has created a space of love within the home. It reflects the extreme nature of our collective crisis that more than ever before in our nation's history, black people participate in the overall assault on the integrity of black single mothers. In the popular mass media, black single mothers are represented as castrating bitches who want to irresponsibly breed children they cannot support. Little distinction is made between working single mothers and women on welfare. They are both unjustly represented as criminals. And the children they parent are represented as would-be criminals. Were there any book written documenting contemporary representation of single mothers in our society, the gap between how white women have been represented (a recent portrayal is that of the hardworking single mom in the film *As Good as It Gets*) and the representation of black women would be clear. White single mothers tend to be represented positively; they are depicted as hardworking victims of circumstances not of their choosing or professional women who at heart are loving madonna figures. Black single mothers are more often than not depicted as neglectful, violent, mentally depraved substance abusers.

Currently the focus on "family values," along with efforts to dismantle welfare, has led to violent condemnation of black single mothers on all fronts. Under the guise of family values, black males have added their voices to the critique of black single mothers. Underlying the attacks on black single mothers is the assumption that patriarchal families are the healthiest. Of course, most of the recent work on nuclear families highlights that these families are more often than not dysfunctional. Feminist scholarship on family life calls attention to the extent to which coercive male domination erodes family values. Widespread domestic violence and male-perpetrated incest are two indications that the patriarchal nuclear family is not inherently a more positive location to raise children than a single-parent household.

Many folks choose to believe that the patriarchal nuclear family is best because they imagine it will be a household with a greater income. Masses of women in this country know that male domination often means that men who head households do not willingly give their money to the support of women and children. In the early part of the twentieth century, the temperance movement exposed the extent to which male patriarchal heads of households withheld money from families to support drinking and carousing. Today, men who earn decent incomes often gamble wages away playing the lottery or engage in substance abuse or womanizing. When the woman in the home also works, patriarchal men are even more inclined to distribute their funds in such a way as to ensure that the family resources will not expand. He may do this by simply deducting from the household funds he once contributed the amount of money that women have made. In two-parent black families where women may make as much money as their mates, if not more, patriarchal men often deploy various strategies to ensure their control of finances.

Studies of patriarchal white families show that when divorce happens, the male heads of households often withhold economic support from women and children. The struggle over household funds can often be such a site of conflict that women of all races and classes simply give in to male demands. These facts can be easily ignored by patriarchal male politicians who want to make it seem as if the presence of men in families means more economic resources and greater emotional stability. Women and children in homes where men withhold their resources know from experience that simply having an adult male present does not mean a better material life or that the household will be a caring and supportive environment.

Amazingly, despite the hardships they face, working black single mothers unequivocally give the bulk of their resources to caring for the welfare of children. This contribution to the material well-being of their children is rarely highlighted. Instead, these mothers must confront sexist stereotypes which deem them castrating matriarchs because they take their parenting roles seriously. Yet it is this high quality of care that makes black single mothers worthy guides for anyone examining the impact of a love ethic in black life. The combination of care, knowledge, respect, and responsibility that is the foundation of loving

CHERISHING SINGLE MOTHERS

practice is clearly evident in the parenting styles of many black single mothers. When black single mothers raise children who become healthy, self-loving, productive citizens, no one calls attention to the strategies they have used to create a positive family life that stands as a complement or alternative to the patriarchal model. We would all like to read studies documenting and highlighting their parenting skills—showing us what they did right.

Instead we hear the most about black single mothers when something has gone wrong in an individual family. While this is even more true if the family receives welfare, the negative fallout impacts on all black single mothers. Ignoring all evidence to the contrary, a vast majority of black male leaders have championed the patriarchal family model. Rarely do they talk about what has motivated fathers to absent themselves from families or to fail to contribute economically. Black males who participated in the Million Man March pledged to assume greater responsibility in families, claiming what some patriarchal men consider their "rightful place as heads of households." They critiqued welfare, but they simply did not talk about the dangerous implications of patriarchal male rule.

Underlying much of the discussion of black male absence from parenting was an implied critique of black females. Sexist black men often suggest that black men are absent because black females have not allowed them to assume their rightful role. Such arguments tend to ignore the reality of black male abandonment and disregard of families. And it in no way examines the extent to which patriarchal black male heads of households have no better track record than their white counterparts when the issue is providing material and emotional care to families. Were more studies done highlighting the actions, behaviors, and values of patriarchal black males who are heads of households and the impact their parenting behavior has on children, we might have a more realistic base from which to determine whether their presence truly enhances the well-being of children.

It should be obvious that all children are likely to be more healthy when raised in a home that is, first and foremost, loving. Homes where there are loving male and female caregivers undoubtedly offer children a positive environment. Yet none of the discussion about the harmful effects of absent black male fathers has centralized love. Instead, patriarchal thinking implies that simply by being present, black fathers ensure that black children will have healthy self-esteem and self-love. This is simply not true. A domineering and/or violently abusive father who is present will not be creating a home environment that promotes a child's well-being. Men do not make life good for women and children by simply being present; it is how they act and interact that makes the difference. Destructive behav-

CHERISHING SINGLE MOTHERS

ior by present black fathers makes black family life dangerous and precarious, just as constructive behavior enhances family life.

By emphasizing the negative, I do not mean to imply that all black fathers are unkind, cruel, or irresponsible. However, if there were a large mass of loving black fathers eager to assume material responsibility for their children and able to provide emotional nurturance, there would be no need to discuss absent fathers, for there would be no problem. Commitment to co-parenting, either when they are present in the home or after the parents break up, would still ensure that black fathers could play a meaningful role in the lives of their children.

Scapegoating single black mothers has allowed black men to deflect attention away from a discussion of the meaning of parenting in their lives. We live in a culture where all men have access to practical, affordable, and adequate forms of birth control. No responsible man need father children he does not want to care for. Until our society stops blaming single mothers, the necessary scholarship that looks at male motives for fathering children that they do not parent will never be undertaken. Concurrently, bashing single mothers does not change the reality that single-parent households are becoming more a norm for all groups. These families are usually headed by women. Rather than negatively stereotyping these families as "at risk" or as pathological, scholars need to highlight single-parent female-headed households that are loving environments.

Significantly, the refusal of our nation to recognize the extraordinary contribution of single mothers who give loving care is tied to the sexist assumption that caregiving is inherently a female trait and not a choice. Yet the fact that some women are from the onset of childbirth unwilling to nurture or give care exposes the fallacy of this myth. While many fathers choose to turn away and abandon children, mothers faced with the same freedom of choice not only stay but do the work of providing economic and emotional stability in the home. That choice is a valuable contribution to family life in our nation. These families are usually no more unstable than those with benevolent patriarchal males present.

Much of the attack on black single mothers has centered on the issue of parenting black boys. When the men's movement first began, its leaders insisted that boys could not be taught how to be men by women, that they needed a male presence. These comments were bandied about without any facts to show that male children raised by single mothers suffer some substantive lack that boys raised in two-parent households do not. Of course, experiential reality does not support this claim. Many of the men, black and nonblack, who have become important leaders in our society, men of wisdom, integrity, and right action, were raised by single mothers. Granted, there are examples of boys raised by single mothers who do not succeed in life, but we see the same problems in boys who had both male and female parental caregivers present. In the case of my own brother, raised in a God-fearing patriarchal home where our mother did not work and our father provided, parental shaming of our brother for being sensitive and gentle, for not being a stellar athlete, was wounding and terribly detrimental to his growth. His temporary fall into irresponsible behavior and addiction was utterly linked to the lack of loving care by our dad. Until this nation can acknowledge that patriarchal fathers who use coercion and other forms of violence to discipline children do not raise healthy, self-loving children, there will be no clear understanding of the value of any male choosing to be a loving parent. Concurrently, when this knowledge is taken into consideration by those who harshly judge single-parent households, the value of women's contribution in raising healthy boys can be fully recognized.

Clearly, females can raise psychologically whole and healthy boys. Single mothers raising children alone seem to understand better than anyone that it is important for their children to have positive, caring interaction with men. Before the breakdown of neighborhood communalism and the formation of the privatized world of housing projects, which isolated poor women and children, there was no black single mother who raised a child without the input of adult male elders and peers. And even in the face of the obstacles privatized housing creates, loving black single mothers make sure that their children have the opportunity to learn from men by interacting with them. They see this as important for both male and female children. Again it must be stated that single mothers welcome the participation of male parental caregivers. There is no evidence to the contrary. However, there is plenty of evidence that men who are dominating and disruptive, who are violent and abusive, are not welcome in healthy female-headed households. Way too many women have internalized guilt about single parenting that has been unjustly placed upon them by our society, and have sought to bring men into the home and keep them there even when the men were disruptive, exploitative, and cruel. These women are merely following the dictates of a society which tells them that the home is a better place if a man is present.

No home is a good environment to raise children in if parents are not loving. There is a big difference between unloving female-headed households and those that are loving. A dysfunctional parent will not create a healthy environment for children. This is as true of the female-headed single-parent household as it is of the male-headed single-parent household. It is equally true of the two-parent household. Children grow best physically and emotionally in homes where they are loved.

Clearly a poor, isolated single female who is not yet emotionally mature, who has not known love, who does not know how to give love to herself or others, will not parent well. Her emotional dysfunctions impede her own growth and make her unable to aid others in their growth. More often than not, young single black females who do not choose pregnancy but through misfortune (failure to use birth control, failure of birth control method, coercive sex) give birth to children they did not want will not parent well. If these mothers receive welfare benefits, they are not allowed to get on-the-job training or experience. As a consequence they may remain caught in a protracted adolescence where they spend the day watching television or doing nothing. They are prime targets for depression and addiction. Their failure to parent well, to create a healthy home environment, is caused neither by their being single nor by their economic status; it is a reflection of their lack of self-development and self-actualization. Raised in the midst of dysfunction, their children often do not learn the necessary skills to grow and prosper in this society; hence a generational cycle of dysfunction is put in place. This is clearly a problem. It will not be solved by simply adding a man into the mix, even if that were possible, which it is

not, for demographics, partnering choices, sexual preferences, incarceration, make this an unrealistic expectation.

Critics of black single mothers insult the intelligence of
families when they suggest that the problems in dysfunctional homes can be solved by men assuming control or
simply by putting an adult male in the home. Usually the
attack on single mothers who receive welfare is aimed
solely at strengthening the position of those political and
economic parties that wish to end state aid. While most
women, particularly those who have received welfare benefits, understand the need for welfare reform, they also
know the importance of having state aid in a society
with severe unemployment problems and no affordable
health care. The primary benefits of welfare have been
housing and health care. While the monetary assistance
women receive is vital to their survival, it is a pittance
compared to the amount that is actually needed for base-
line maintenance of a household. I always think that the
men who speak so eloquently against welfare, many of
whom have children that they do not parent even if they
contribute economically, should have to maintain a household for a month on state aid while being caregivers.
Despite the reality of child abuse in all families, irrespective of class, and especially in dysfunctional poor and
utterly destitute families, it is remarkable that children do

not die from the sheer misery and hardship they are forced to endure.

If black leaders, mostly male, continue to ignore the valuable contributions to the stability of black family life made by caring single mothers, they will undermine and ultimately destroy the valuable and essential contributions single mothers make as they strive to create healthy homes for themselves and their children. Obviously, given the odds against them, many single mothers give adequate care but are unable to fully create an ideal home life. All praise is due working single black mothers and their comrades receiving state aid who manage, in the face of adversity and circumstances they cannot change, to create loving home environments. They need to be given grants to write the guides for their dysfunctional counterparts and for everyone parenting under circumstances that are not ideal. These women are seers with wisdom to share with our communities and the nation about the nature of love. Unrecognized and unappreciated, they do the work of loving every day.

*Eight*

# loving black masculinity—
# fathers, lovers, friends

I N MY MEMOIR of my childhood, *Bone Black,* the section about my grandfather begins: "His smells fill my nostrils with the scent of happiness. With him all the broken pieces of my heart get mended, put together again bit by bit." My mother's father, Daddy Gus, was an incredibly gentle and kind human being. A quiet man with no harsh words, a respected deacon of his church, he bestowed on me the unconditional love that provided me with a psychological basis to trust in the goodness of men. He was not a patriarch. Married to Baba, our grandmother, for more than seventy years, he was also present in our lives, in the lives of his children. When he was on his deathbed, he expressed love and devotion to Baba. He had been what the preacher called one of the right-hand men of God, a good and faithful servant of the divine.

My dad, Mr. Veodis, is a patriarchal man. Like my grandfather, he is a respected deacon at his church. He is also a quiet man, but that is where the resemblance ends. My daddy is a man capable of harsh words and harsh actions. He was raised in a household where his daddy was not present, and he only came to know him fully late in life. Throughout our childhood he was a stern protector and provider. Being manly meant that he eschewed any concern with love. According to patriarchal standards, he is "much of a man." As a parental caregiver Dad has always conformed to the patriarchal ideal. He has been a present father, parenting seven children (six girls and one boy) and always bringing home the bacon. He has been for most of our lives emotionally unavailable. As a patriarchal man he always held to the belief that the tending to house and home, to the needs of children, is woman's work. Now that he is almost eighty, Daddy has become more emotionally engaging. With his grandchildren he is tender and caring, present to them in ways that he was never present to us.

Our brother was from the start a disappointment to Dad. Like Daddy Gus, our brother is by nature kind and gentle. He is not a man of harsh words or harsh actions.

While he liked sports as a boy, he was just not that interested in being a major sports figure. Our father had been a soldier and gone to war. We had pictures of him playing basketball, of him in the boxing ring, pictures of him with his all-black infantry unit. My brother was bad at sports. He was a disappointment to our dad, and as punishment Dad withheld from him affection and affirmation.

In the world I grew up in, adult black males were present in most homes; like my dad, they were providers and protectors. Mama's brothers were a constant presence in our lives and in the lives of their children. They were caring, funny, supportive. Mama loved her father and her brothers. My dad's father, Daddy Jerry, was also a beloved presence in our childhood. We did not know then that he had not been present in our father's life when he was a boy. We knew only that Dad had been raised as the only child of a stern and demanding mother. His childhood had not been easy. He had always worked hard. There was so much diverse black masculinity in the world of our childhood that it would have been impossible for any of us to have a one-dimensional understanding of black life. We knew from experience that some black males were kind and gentle, others cruel and indifferent, that some fathers were present and some fathers were absent. All our segregated institutions were led by benevolent black male patriarchs, men who were respected and admired.

Coming from this environment, when I reached college at the beginning of the seventies, I was stunned by the way black men were described in novels and sociological and psychological literature. From these books I learned that black men were irresponsible, lazy, and unwilling to assume responsibility for their families, that even when black men wanted to be providers and protectors of their families they could not be because they were "castrated." I can still remember looking up the word "castration" in the dictionary and mulling over its meaning: "to render impotent by psychological means." My astonishment deepened when I learned that matriarchal black women had been the ones to emasculate and castrate black men. Initially, I found this material amusing because it was so absolutely ludicrous, in no way conforming to my own experience. Initially, it just seemed like the twisted fictions of white supremacy.

Our father had always been acutely aware of the way in which white supremacist thinking and action subordinated black men. He let us know early on that the white man did not want the black man to be a man, so he tried to keep him down by denying him jobs, by encouraging him to act like a boy. Mr. Veodis was proud that he was "nobody's boy." This critical backdrop provided me with the necessary information to interrogate and challenge the material I was taught in college. Clearly the perspectives on black masculinity I was studying had been shaped by racist thinking, by myths and stereotypes. It did not take long for me to realize that those academic discussions of black masculinity based on real-life studies highlighted the experiences of poor urban black males and made that the representative norm. In these studies there was no diverse black masculinity, no wide range of options a black male might choose from to define self and world.

The men of my father's generation, born and raised in periods of intense racial apartheid, were far more politicized about racism and imperialism than the young black males I met at college. These young men were far more likely to blame black women than white supremacy for keeping the black man down. This was a far cry from the days when Daddy would come home from work and I would hear him greet our black male neighbor, who worked in the mines, "Ain't nothing to it, white man running it." There was no day in Daddy's life and in the lives of his hardworking mates that they were not acutely aware of racial injustice and its impact on their lives. These black men did not see themselves as the special victims of white supremacy; they knew it hurt all black people. They had been among the first black men to fight for this country in foreign wars. They had been treated with hatred and contempt. They were expected to die for a country that would not let them live as men. They knew who the enemy was, and it was not their laziness (they knew that they were not lazy because they worked long hard hours every day). They also knew that black women were not the enemy because these were the arms that embraced and nurtured them when they returned home from fighting the white man's war, from working in the white man's world.

Generations of black men who came after my dad, men like my brother, had to some extent been shielded from the hatred and contempt of the white world in ways that their fathers had not. These young black men did not live with the day-to-day fear that they would be lynched or shot on the spot, with impunity for the shooter, if they got out of their place. Yet these contemporary young black men had and have a level of discontent and rage that was and is far deeper than the anger of their fathers because their expectations were and are greater. All the gains of the civil rights struggle had led them to feel that they were entitled to everything this country had to offer, every benefit, every privilege. They felt they were more entitled to privileges than black women, or for that matter any group of women, because they had been sent by the country to wars. They were expected to give their life for the country and they expected the country to give something back to them.

Patriarchal thinking fueled black male rage at the end of the sixties and the beginning of the seventies. This new generation of young black patriarchs had never suffered the abuses their fathers and grandfathers had known, yet they were more inclined to weep and moan and expect their tears would be wiped away. They were willing to play the role of victim to the hilt if it meant that they could get over. Unlike their black male ancestors, they were fundamentally opportunistic. Elaine Brown's memoir, *A Taste of Power*, painfully documents the extent to which many young black males leading the militant black power struggle were psychologically confused. Obsessed with grandiose visions of power, they were willing to engage in coercive domination as a way of asserting control and gaining power. While militant black male leaders challenged white supremacy in productive ways, their uncritical embrace of patriarchy undermined anti-racist struggle by falsely projecting the idea that black women were the enemies of black men.

Unlike the generations of hardworking patriarchal black men who had preceded them, they passively accepted the white man's account of black masculinity and made it their own. They did not want to be like their fathers. Nathan McCall attests to this fact in his memoir, *Makes Me Wanna Holler*: "I never heard my friends say they wanted to be like their fathers when they grew up. Why would we want that when we knew our fathers were catching hell? That would be like saying we wanted to catch hell, too. If anything we wanted to be the opposite of our fathers. We didn't want to work for the white man and end up like them." This was the mind-set that led new generations of black males to accept the racist notion that their fathers were not "real" men and with it the idea that black women were somehow in cahoots with white men to keep the black man down.

At all other moments in our history black males and females had recognized that we were in the struggle together. It was assumed that part of what freedom would ultimately bring was a lifestyle where all black men could be patriarchs and keep their women subordinate. To my father it was a mark of pride that Mama did not work when we were growing up. Now and then when she did little jobs to buy luxuries for her children, he was not pleased and felt she was indulging us. Believing that hard work creates discipline, he felt it was important that we learn as children to sacrifice and work hard. My brother did not share this work ethic. He wanted life to be easy. When it was not, he and the males of his generation looked for someone to blame. Our father and the black men of his generation always knew white supremacy was the problem, not black women. When the younger generation of black males could not blame everything on white racism, they targeted black women.

By the early seventies many young black males had begun to denounce black women as traitors. Falling into

SALVATION

line with the thinking of the Moynihan report, which suggested that a black matriarchy existed which disempowered black men, they began to suggest that black women should be more subordinate if black men were to assume their rightful place as patriarchs. Love was not the issue, the issue was their ongoing homosocial war with white men. When Eldridge Cleaver published *Soul on Ice,* he was not denouncing racist/sexist stereotypes that labeled all black men rapists. Embracing the identity of rapist, he bragged about raping black women as practice for raping white women. Cleaver, and the black males who thought as he did, were conducting a war with white men over who could be the real man, the hard man, the big dick. In the wake of the contemporary feminist movement, black males were daring white men to stand up and celebrate patriarchal masculinity rooted in woman-hating. Cleaver, and other self-declared militant black male leaders, said nothing about love.

Importantly, we need to remember that it was a white-male-dominated publishing industry which printed and sold *Soul on Ice.* While white male patriarchs were pretending to respond to the demands of the feminist movement, they were allowing and even encouraging black males to give voice to violent woman-hating sentiments. Since black males were portrayed as victims, castrated and emasculated, white and black women alike were especially

136

forgiving of black male sexism. When individual black women active in the feminist movement challenged black male misogyny, we were attacked as traitors to the race. The publication of Michele Wallace's *Black Macho and the Myth of the Superwoman* was the first major attempt by a black woman to critique black male woman-hating.

It was tacitly assumed that were black males able to gain access to the patriarchal privileges that had for the most part been denied them, they would love themselves. If they regained their lost manhood, with it would come an intact self-esteem and self-love. Tragically, black men did not win the war against white male patriarchs. Our leaders were assassinated and imprisoned. The movement that had begun with a bang ended with a whimper. While many lives had been lost, black people were not free. Without militant warfare, white women were gaining rights and access to jobs that had been denied black people. The ascendancy of white women, who were winning their fight for equal rights with men of their class, seemed to intensify black men's rage, and they gave public voice to fierce woman-hating. These young men disrespected and deval-ued black women's place in freedom struggles. Their newly found manhood could only be affirmed when they could subordinate women.

On the manhood front, the image of the militant black prince fighting for his freedom was soon replaced by the get-over playboy image of the daddy mack, "the pimp." Unable to sustain a competitive patriarchal masculinity in the world of work, where control was still in white hands, many patriarchal black men looked to the sexual arena as the place where they could salvage wounded self-esteem. While they might not possess the political and economic power of patriarchal white men, they could outdo them on the sexual front. When it came to sex, they could win. Books like *Gentlemen of Leisure: A Year in the Life of a Pimp* extolled the rewards of exploiting women, white and black, to get over. Embracing sexual images that were racist/sexist and dehumanizing gave black men the license to use and abuse black women. It created division between the sexes in ways that undermined anti-racist struggle.

Once the image of the playboy was projected as desirable, it became more acceptable for black males to father children and assume no responsibility for parenting. The black men of my father's generation aspired to be benevolent patriarchs, men who would provide for and protect the women and children in their families. They would be heads of households who did not need to use force or coercion to dominate. While they saw women as different and even inferior, they did not condone the use of force to subordinate females. Nonbenevolent patriarchs shared the assumption that women were different and inferior, but they also saw females as evil and treacherous. They were invested in woman-hating. They ruled by coercion and domination. This was the masculinity the pimp embodied; it was represented in movies as glamorous and powerful. And this is the masculinity young black men are increasingly embracing. Misogynist rap and woman-hating hip-hop culture continues to encourage black males to hate women, and to see being sexual predators as "cool." When progressive hip-hop spokesperson Kevin Powell critiques black male sexism, he is often ridiculed by unenlightened male and female peers. His insightful, powerful essay "Confessions of a Recovering Misogynist" breaks new ground by creating the space for young black males and females to constructively confront sexism by changing their attitudes and behavior.

Hardcore pimp masculinity did not and does not place value on love. The playboy guy was not interested in getting married and having a family. Published in the seventies, Barbara Ehrenreich's book on masculinity, *The Hearts of Men: American Dreams and the Flight from Commitment,* called attention to the widespread white male embrace of playboy masculinity. The new playboy was out to have fun and was willing to use and abuse women in the process. His value and worth was determined by his capacity to seduce women. Children and family were not important. While conservative whites targeted black masculinity, labeling it unstable and irresponsible, they did not launch a critique of the white playboy. As the aging, mostly white playboys gave up their fun and married, black males who embraced pimp masculinity tried to be players forever. If they married, their relationships were torn apart by infidelity and betrayal. White male playboys legitimized the rejection of fatherhood, but when this stance was embraced by black males it had disastrous implications for black family life.

Contrary to popular racist/sexist myths, so-called matriarchal black women did not create instability in black families. Often the black family was first destabilized by the presence of disappointed, angry black fathers and then by absent fathers. In *Makes Me Wanna Holler,* Nathan McCall courageously makes the point that bitter, angry fathers do not create happy households: "That's why I shake my head when I hear so-called social experts harping on the problems of black single-parent households. They don't seem to understand that the problems go deeper than that. A two-parent home is not better off than a single-parent one if the father is fucked up in the head and beaten down. There's nothing more dangerous and destructive in a household than a frustrated, oppressed black man." Since conventional patriarchal thinking had socialized women and men in this society to see parenting as a female task, there was no uproar about black males abdicating parenting roles.

In the 1980s, as more white men also sought to escape marriage and family, books like Dan Kiley's *The Peter Pan Syndrome: Men Who Have Never Grown Up* voiced cultural alarm. Yet his work focused solely on white men, even though its basic ideas described many black males. Kiley's argument was that young boys were learning that growing up meant that they had to work hard and become benevolent patriarchs caring and providing for others. The Peter Pan syndrome emerges when a boy decides he wants to stay young forever and spend his life partying and having fun. Kiley maintained: "Irresponsibility is a key to staying young." In black communities men had the added advantage of blaming their irresponsible behavior on the system's failure to provide jobs.

Since the tenets of patriarchal masculinity upheld the notion that it was not manly to parent lovingly, most unemployed black men did not spend their leisure time with children. They spent time with their male buddies. Despite a huge body of critical writing about the importance of fathers, patriarchal thinking still encourages women and men to believe that paternal contribution to parenting is never as important as that of mothers. Naturally a culture that teaches everyone that fathers exist to provide material sustenance places no value on the emotional nurturance of fathers. This has been especially true in black life.

When I decided I wanted to have a child, my black male partner at the time felt he was not ready for fatherhood. Since I believe children should be desired by both parents, I respected his decision. Sharing this information with women friends of all races, I was stunned by their insistence that if I wanted a baby I should have one and ignore his wishes. These sentiments were shocking to me given how much we know about the ways children suffer when fathers are uncaring and indifferent. Contrary to what we are told about absent fathers, the focus on whether fathers are present in the home really tends to overlook the more important issue, which is father love. As long as our society devalues the importance of male emotional nurturance and love, children will be denied healthy relationships with fathers. All children need to have positive connections to people of both genders. And children desire connections with fathers as much as they do with mothers. This does not mean that children who have fathers present in the home are necessarily more healthy.

Clearly, many children who are raised without fathers can and do grow to be healthy, mature adults. This does not mean that they do not have grief about their absent fathers. In *Whatever Happened to Daddy's Little Girl*, Jonetta Rose Barros explores the pain of fatherless daughters. She contends: "A girl abandoned by the first man in her life forever entertains powerful feelings of being unworthy or incapable of receiving any man's love. Children raised in the most loving lesbian families often still yearn to know about their fathers. When the knowledge they are given is truthful and reassuring they do not feel psychologically damaged. Father love helps to create a foundation for healthy self-esteem among children."

It is psychologically damaging to children when fathers are not loving. Most black fathers are rarely completely absent from a child's life. They may appear and disappear. The issue again is what they give when they are present. Way too many black fathers give nothing when they are present because society has told them, and everyone else, either that the emotional contributions of men have no meaning or that to be real men they must withhold affection, affirmation, and love. In our family, the one boy was damaged not because Daddy was not present but because he always treated his son with contempt and disdain, undermining his self-esteem and his self-confidence. This is common in patriarchal family life. Most of the contributors to the anthology *Father Songs: Testimonies by African-American Sons and Daughters* share stories of emotional and/or physical abuse from fathers. In some cases fathers were present in the family only for a day, a week, or a month but in that short time managed to wreak emotional havoc and in some cases wound and scar children for life.

SALVATION

A central component of patriarchal thinking is that it is the male role to discipline children. In many homes such thinking has sanctioned cruel physical punishment of children by adult men. Since women also are socialized to accept patriarchal thinking, lots of women believe that a man is performing his proper role when he acts as an authoritarian disciplinarian. In recent years, black male thinkers and leaders have joined with conservative white voices to attack female-headed households and to proclaim the need for a male presence. Yet rarely do these men talk about the substantive qualities black men should bring to their role as parents. None of these men talk about the art of loving.

If all the critics of black family life who stress the importance of black male presence focused on the issue of love, they could not insist, as they do, that boys need fathers more than girls do. In her memoir, *Laughing in the Dark,* Patrice Gaines shares the insight that "fathers are just as important to girls as to boys. . . . Some fathers, like mine, are absent even when they are present. . . . My deepest self knew that before I went out into the world and found a man to love I needed to be loved by the first man in my life. I needed a rich and basic love by which to judge the love of all other men." Gaines, like so many of us, never got the affirmation of her value from her father that she longed for. When fathers are present and uncaring or cruel, they do damage. A father who seldom sees a child but gives love contributes more to that child's emotional growth than a father who is present but always indifferent, who shames, coerces, and engages in all manner of abusive behavior.

Everyone in our culture is reluctant to talk about the importance of father love. The moment we place love on the agenda we have to talk about all the forces in our society that keep us from being loving, from loving ourselves and others. Loving fathers do not abandon families. Hence if our entire culture taught all men the art of loving, we would not have the problem of absent fathers. Within white supremacist capitalist patriarchy, black males who embrace the values of these ideologies have enormous difficulty with the issue of self-love. Patriarchal thinking certainly does not encourage men to be self-loving. Instead it encourages them to believe that power is more important than love, particularly the power to dominate and control others.

Most men in our society are more obsessed with masculinity than with the issue of whether or not they are loving. Frank Pittman writes in *Man Enough:* "The great passion in a man's life may not be for women or men or wealth or toys or fame, or even for his children, but for his masculinity, and at any point in his life he may be tempted to throw over the things for which he regularly lays down his life, for the sake of that masculinity." This has been all too true for most black men. Every day of our lives black men are killing one another to prove their masculinity. Understanding the implication of this, black male poet Essex Hemphill constantly challenged the sexist projection of black women as the enemies of black men. In a conversation with Isaac Julien published in the anthology *Speak My Name,* he shared: "It's important to realize it isn't black women who are gunning down one another. Black women are not gunning us down and beating us to death. We are doing this." Tragically, black male obsession with masculinity is the barrier keeping individual black men from learning how to love themselves and others.

Loving black males find their way to love by letting go of patriarchal thinking which insists that they be defined by what they do with their penis, or by how brutal, mean, and dominating they can be toward someone else. Feminist thinking is useful to black males, and all males, who are grappling with the issue of self-love because it offers strategies that enable them to challenge and change patriarchal masculinity. It offers to men a vision of liberatory masculinity. In most families males are taught to dislike their bodies, to disconnect from them, to believe that they have some uncontrollable sexuality that will get them into trouble. All such thinking undermines a young male's self-esteem and self-confidence. In black life, males often learn on the one hand to overidentify with the penis and on the other hand to see the penis, and sexuality, in general as the enemy of their well-being. This then sets the stage for scapegoating and blaming women, whether they be mothers or lovers.

As part of his process of developing a feminist consciousness, Kevin Powell reflects on and describes this scapegoating in *Keepin' It Real:* "I remembered hating my mother and blaming her for everything terrible in my life: my father's absence, the poverty, the depth with which I hated myself. I remembered how the boys and men in my neighborhood used to talk to their mothers and sisters and girlfriends and wives. More often than not they would belittle or insult those women or blame them for their problems." When black males stop blaming women or any force outside their control for their inability to take responsibility for their lives, they are on the path to self-love and healing.

While he does not explore the issue deeply, Kevin Powell does raise the useful point that his mother often took total responsibility for all his needs and as a consequence he did not learn the skills for basic care. Dan Kiley identified this as one of the symptoms of the Peter Pan syndrome. Black mothers, like other women in patriarchal society, often feel they are fulfilling their rightful role by serving males, whether they are husbands or sons. It is not unusual to hear young black boys make demands for service from grandmothers, mothers, and sisters, and it is often seen as a sign of healthy masculinity. In reality the male who never learns how to take care of his basic needs is infantilized. Mothers who indulge sons and allow them to be irresponsible are not being loving. Their actions are motivated by the desire to bind the boy to them. This is a context that breeds emotional incest, which is as dangerous to a boy's self-esteem as physical incest. We have all heard black males praise their mothers and fault all the other women in their lives who do not subordinate their needs to his the way his mama did.

Contrary to popular myth, boys raised in single-parent female-headed households are usually taught patriarchal thinking in these homes. Often it is their mothers who teach them that women should be subordinate to men, that by virtue of maleness they should have more power and privilege. When patriarchal society affirms this truth, mothers' disrespect is echoed. They, and other women, can be blamed as the source of males' unhappiness and failure in life.

The flip side of the indulgent subordinated mother who bends over backward to meet her son's every need is the domineering, verbally and/or physically abusive mother who uses shaming and constant humiliation as a means of disciplining male children. Insightfully, in *The Mermaid and the Minotaur* Dorothy Dinnerstein links this early adult female domination of the boy child to a penchant for male violence against women in later life. In two-parent houses where adult males degrade mothers, boys who witness this may be overwhelmed by guilt and spend their lives trying to give their mother the care she has been denied. In all homes, be they single- or two-parent households, boys are damaged when mothers force them to be symbolic partners. While they may strive to satisfy the mom, they feel rage and resentment that they are placed in this position.

All the single mothers, black and nonblack, who raise healthy sons who later become mature, responsible men capable of giving and receiving love know that it is a lie that only men can raise sons. Patriarchal culture currently seeks to devalue single mothers by insisting they cannot raise healthy sons, even though there is no documentation to show this truth. All the data we have available documents the fact that loving single mothers can and do parent sons who are as healthy as those in two-parent households. Dysfunctional households rarely produce psychologically healthy boys whether they are single- or two-parent households. When the focus is on black life and the parenting of boys, mainstream culture likes to insist that only black men can raise healthy boys. Underlying this insistence is the assumption that these boys need coercive discipline which only a black male authority figure can

give. All these assumptions about the needs of black boys
are informed by racist and sexist stereotypes which identify these children as dangerous threats to the safety of
everyone else, whose spirits must be tamed or broken early
in life. Tragically, more and more black people endorse
and support this line of thought. No public leaders talk
about black boys needing healthy love, which necessarily
includes teaching children how to be disciplined along
with other life-enhancing skills.

Whose interest does it really serve to instill in the public's imagination that only black men can raise a healthy
black male child in a society where so many black males
refuse to engage in parenting? Following this logic would
lead to the assumption that all black males raised in
female-headed houses are unhealthy and dysfunctional.
Certainly such thinking does not serve the interests of
black boys or the women who provide them with parental
care. While it is clear that black boys, and all children, need
positive connections with adult men, those men do not
have to be fathers. It is also clear that a woman alone can
raise a healthy boy child. For too long, single mothers of all
races have been made to feel that the lack of male parental
influence is their fault. No one has prevented black males
or any group of males from parenting their children. There
is no evidence to support the notion that healthy mothers
try to keep healthy fathers away from sons or daughters.

The hard truth that this nation does not want to face is that most patriarchal men, irrespective of their racial identity, do not wish to be loving parental caretakers.

Attacks on black single mothers raising sons are rooted in woman-hating. They make all single mothers feel that they are failing sons if they cannot bring a father presence into the home. Or they make mothers fear they will harm their sons by loving them. Pittman suggests: "The single mother and her fatherless son may fear that her love will hurt her son. She may pull back from him, and thus withdraw the only parenting the boy ever got. In protecting him from what she believes to be her dangerous love, she may inadvertently turn him into an orphan." When this happens boys suffer. In *The Courage to Raise Good Men*, therapist Olga Silverstein says: "In the name of being a good mother sometimes we sacrifice our very beliefs about right and wrong, abandoning our sons to the prevailing culture." Healthy mothers and fathers know that the patriarchal vision of masculinity puts their sons at risk. While it may help them grow into acceptable "macho" men capable of being hard, it will not teach them how to know who they are, be responsible, and be able to love. Black mothers raising nonsexist sons in patriarchal culture must work doubly hard to counter negative messages about masculinity and female leadership.

Opposing patriarchal notions of masculinity is one way

to support boys and men in their efforts to be self-loving. Olga Silverstein identifies the good man as one who "will be empathic and strong, autonomous and connected, responsible to self, to family and friends, and to society, and capable of understanding how those responsibilities are, ultimately, inseparable." All my life I have had an opportunity to know the love of caring "good" black men. In each case these men are individuals who have dared to break with conventional macho masculinity and care for their souls and their inner life. When black males internalize the values of white supremacist capitalist patriarchy they deny their need to love and be loved. Mature decolonized black men know love is the healing force that allows true freedom. They know that loving males and females, together or alone, can chart the path to self-actualization for black boys and lost black men seeking to find their way home.

Jarvis Jay Masters is a loving black male confined to death row. Using this time of enforced solitude to explore the interiors of his mind and heart, he came to the realization that many inmates were victims of extreme child abuse, sharing: "Throughout my many years of institutionalization, I, like so many of these men, unconsciously took refuge behind prison walls. Not until I read a series of books for adults who had been abused as children did I become committed to the process of examining my own childhood." The child of a drug-addicted mother and a violent stepfather, who at four witnessed the death of his baby brother, Masters realized that he, like other black men, did not fear prison because it is a place that "welcomes a man who is full of rage and violence." By learning self-love, Masters practiced forgiveness and compassion. When his mother died, his fellow inmates could not understand his longing to have been with her, because she had neglected him. Being self-loving, he responded, "But am I to neglect myself as well by denying that I wished I'd been with her when she died, that I still love her." Masters shows that it is never to late for black males to learn the art of loving. Stevie Wonder often sings the lyrics "I want to know what love is. I want you to show me." Free black men know love.

*Nine*

# heterosexual love—
# union and reunion

THERE HAS NEVER been a time in this nation when the bonds of love between black women and men have not been under siege. If slavery was not an institution powerful enough to destroy the ties that unite and bind us, we have every reason to hope that bonds of love, of union and reunion, will be ever possible between us. However, this does not mean that heterosexual relationships between black women and men are not in crisis; they are. Talk to any black person who was active in the sixties' struggles for black liberation and they will recall that the most packed meetings were those focusing on black male–female relationships. Those were the days when astute black leaders acknowledged the need for there to be ongoing critical discussion about heterosexual bonds.

Bonds of affection and love that are forged in the midst of profound trauma and oppression have a resiliency that can inspire and sustain generations. Our history as black people can never be marked solely by the experience of enslavement; instead it must be marked by the fusion of circumstance between the free and the bound. Even though there were only a small number of free black folks who chose to immigrate to this so-called New World, their presence had a profound impact on the imagination of the masses who were enslaved. Imagine how just the sight of or knowledge of one free black person would have gripped the imagination of any enslaved individual. Among that small group of black folks who had migrated to the Americas by choice and not by coercion, black males were the majority group, free black females were few. Any black male, free or slave, who wanted to have a union with a black woman had to confront the reality of slavery and indentured servitude.

Historically, all unions between black women and men were forged within a culture of white supremacy wherein all bonding which did not serve the interests of white people was deemed suspect and threatening. No group of black people knew better than the slaves that positive union between black women and men threatened white supremacist claims on black bodies. Free and enslaved black folks fought hard to privilege these relationships by rituals and ceremony, both illegal and legal, because they recognized that solidifying these bonds, gaining public recognition of their value, was crucial to the freedom struggle. Reading accounts of heterosexual black relationships during slavery reveals the extent to which the desire to create long-standing domestic partnerships, whether through marriage or shacking (living together without benefit of clergy), often served as the catalyst inspiring individuals to fiercely resist bondage and work for freedom. Importantly, remembering that white supremacist thinking is always challenged by loving unions between black males and females sheds light on why there have been so many obstacles placed in the path of such unions.

Socialized within the context of the United States to believe that men should be dominant and women subservient, the vast majority of African-Americans have held in high esteem a patriarchal vision of family life. Despite the fact that the systematic institutionalization of white supremacy and everyday racism made it impossible for the vast majority of African-Americans to create family life based on the sexist assumption that men should be providers working to sustain the material needs of the family and women nurturers taking care of emotional needs and the concerns of the household, black people have worked hard to conform to this model. Even when our lived experience indicated that the model of communal kinship with gender equality was both more constructive and more realistic in a world where employment was and is hard to find for any black person, most black folks continue to accept patriarchal notions of sex roles as the standard to judge and evaluate black life. I can remember my mother expressing a desire to try and find work so that my father, who worked hard as a janitor, would not have to bear all the economic burdens of our household, but he was adamant that no wife of his needed to work, even if that meant material lack. To him, supporting his wife and family affirmed his manhood. This affirmation took precedence over material needs.

Of course the patriarchal idea that men should rule over women did not promote gender equity or love between black women and men. All too often heterosexual relationships based on sexist norms in black life were places where men felt satisfied and women dissatisfied. Male domination does not lead to happy homes, no matter all the propaganda that suggests otherwise. Even in the most benevolent patriarchal households women often feel unloved. When I was a child I often heard adult black females disparage black men for not embracing the role of patriarchal provider. And while there were some men who were prevented from assuming this role because they lacked employment, there were also men who were gainfully employed who did not choose to offer their money to support wives and children. Every black woman I knew growing up dreamed of having a black male partner who would give her financial support and allow her to be a housewife. Of course the reality of class and race politics made it all but impossible for these fantasies to be fulfilled (if there were no jobs for the vast majority of black men, how could they assume the role of providers). The failure of black men to fulfill these fantasies created rage in many black females. That rage intensified as employment opportunities increased, as more black males found work but remained unwilling to assume the provider role.

No research has been done on black males who work, who live in households with wives and children, but refuse to give their income to be providers. Daily we are bombarded with messages in mass media which tell us black women are these strong matriarchs who enjoy being the heads of households, when the reality remains that very few black women have had a choice. Indeed, just as black females often feel rage that black men do not deliver the economic goods, black men often feel enraged that they are expected to provide. The economic realities of black heterosexual life are rarely given proper attention in our society, even though struggles over money are a primary reason couples divorce, irrespective of race. Given the ongoing crisis of employment in black life, these struggles are more intensified. One in three black folks lives in poverty—and half of all black children. Black people who have the same educational background as whites can expect to make 82 to 86 percent of the income of whites. Yet no one talks about how economic injustice creates a context for emotional strife in domestic households.

For years now this nation has acknowledged that black men—and, for that matter, all groups of men who are unable to provide for their families—often feel as though they are emasculated. That is all the more the case if the women in their lives are able to find work when the men cannot. Of course patriarchal thinking presents this news to the public as though it is not only natural for men to want to provide economically for the needs of others but equally natural for men to feel castrated and depressed if they are deprived of access to the jobs that would enable them to be providers. While it is true that partriarchal socialization teaches men that their value lies with work and providing for others, it is also true that many men have long resisted this socialization. Masses of men, many of them white, have high-paying jobs yet withhold financial support from wives and children. These men do not seem to feel at all "castrated" because they are failing to assume the provider role.

Men who provide economically in heterosexual unions are much more likely to use this as a means of exerting power and control over others in the household. Indeed, the notion that black men were castrated was rooted in the assumption that more often than not black women were bringing home the bulk of the family income. Until feminist movement interrogated the notion that men should be the sole providers of families and changed the way we all think about the nature of work, some black men did feel that they could not assume their rightful role as provider. This led them to feel depressed and hostile toward black women who provided. The myth of the black matriarchy falsely projected the idea that black women were castrating black men by being dominant. Created and projected onto black life by a white supremacist patriarchal culture that did not want to assume accountability for the way in which racialized economic injustice assaulted black male self-esteem, the myth was used to encourage black men to enter the military and there regain their wounded and/or lost masculinity. It was definitely a strategic move for white male patriarchs to scapegoat and blame black women, encouraging black males to do the same, because such thinking disrupted the bonds of solidarity that had been forged between black women and men working together to resist racism.

No work really documents the extent to which post–

civil rights uncritical acceptance of patriarchal thinking by black males wreaked havoc in black family life. When sex roles in black life did not conform to sexist patterns, black women and men often forged new paradigms of love and affection. From slavery on, black males (and most black females) had theoretically accepted the same sexism that was the norm in the dominant white patriarchy, but material deprivation caused by exploitation and oppression based on race and class meant that gender roles in black life could not conform to sexist norms. Black women were workers. Unemployed or marginally employed black men often cooked, cleaned, and did child care. The fact that black women worked outside the home and worked equally hard as black men in the anti-racist struggle was not seen as detrimental to the psychological welfare of the black family but central to its survival. Gender equity among black women and men, however unchosen and relative, did not create a lack of love between couples, for everyone understood that solidarity was needed to ensure survival.

Congressman and civil rights activist John Lewis tells the story of his parents' marriage in his memoir of the movement, *Walking with the Wind*. Married in 1932 to a sharecropper, his mother had no honeymoon with her husband because there was neither time nor money. Lewis recalls: "After Eddie married my mother, they both joined the Lewis family in Lula's house, and my mother began working with them in those fields, sometimes side by side with her husband, other times 'working out' for one local farmer or another, chopping or picking cotton for fifty cents a day." Whether or not a black woman would work was not a realistic option for most black families. Her economic contribution was desperately needed. Love flourished in situations where black women and men worked together mutually to sustain their bonds and to nurture families.

Without feminist thinking undergirding the alternative gender arrangements black couples had to make in order to ensure material survival, even when they were productive and fruitful these arrangements were often regarded as "wrong" by women and men alike. Most working black women longed for a time when they would be able to rely on their men to be the sole providers. Many white women did not understand this, and when the contemporary feminist movement began, it hailed work as the key to liberation and labeled black women already liberated. In reality most black women knew that they were not at all liberated by backbreaking low-wage labor. Working menial jobs where they were subjected to degradation and sexual harassment by racist white employers did not enhance black women's self-esteem. Significantly, during the early stages of feminist movement, Gallup polls showed black males to be the group of men most supportive of gender equity in the workforce.

When militant black male leaders dominating the anti-racist movement made freedom synonymous with the subordination of black women, their uncritical embrace of the notion that black men had been symbolically castrated was not challenged by men. Individual black women active in anti-racist struggle and in what was then called "women's liberation" interrogated these myths and rightly refused to accept any notion that they were the oppressors of black men. Clearly, the widespread acceptance of the idea that black women were the "enemy" created more havoc in black life than any other idea. That havoc is well documented in the 1970 anthology *The Black Woman.* Reprinted in this anthology was a 1966 essay by Abbey Lincoln, "Who Will Revere the Black Woman." Lincoln wrote: "But strange as it is, I've heard it echoed by too many Black full-grown males that Black womanhood is the downfall of the Black man in that she (the Black woman) is 'evil,' 'hard to get along with,' 'domineering,' 'suspicious,' and 'narrow-minded.' In short, a black, ugly, evil you-know-what." Like her progressive black women comrades, Lincoln called attention to the way in which this thinking justified sexist black male use of coercion and abuse as a means to subordinate and/or dominate black women. She identified the extent to which domestic violence and rape were becoming a norm in black life.

Echoing Lincoln's sentiments in her essay "The Black Woman As a Woman," Kay Lindsay asserted: "Those who are exerting their 'manhood' by telling Black women to step back into a domestic, submissive role are assuming a counter-revolutionary position. Black women likewise have been abused by the system and we must begin talking about the elimination of all kinds of oppression." In her insightful essay "On the Issue of Roles," Toni Cade Bambara went to the heart of the matter and critiqued both black males and females for regarding each other through negative sexist stereotypes. Emphasizing the importance of liberation struggle as the "measure of womanhood," she urged recognition of the need to affirm progressive gender roles, stating: "Invariably I hear from some dude that Black women must be supportive and patient so that Black men can regain their manhood. The notion of womanhood, they argue—and only if pressed to address themselves to the notion do they think of it or argue—is dependent on his defining his manhood. . . . And I wonder if the dudes who keep hollering about their lost balls realized that they probably surrendered them either to Mr. Charlie in the marketplace, trying to get that Eldorado, or to Miss Anne in bed, trying to bang out some sick notion of love and freedom. It seems to me that you find your Self in destroying illusions, smashing myths, laundering the head of whitewash, being responsible to some truth, to the struggle. That entails at the very least cracking through the veneer of this sick society's definition of 'masculine' and 'feminine.' " Bambara and her progressive black women colleagues worked hard to call attention to the destructive fallout caused by hard-core black male support of patriarchal thinking, but their words did not have widespread impact.

In actuality, large numbers of sexist black women were as willing to embrace the notion that they should be more subordinate or at least act the part as were black men. Since black women did not then join together in unity to support the need for progressive visions of gender roles in black life, the stage was set for conflict between females. When younger women like myself embraced feminist thinking, we were often seen as traitors to the race and judged harshly by black males and females alike. At the peak of feminist movement Michele Wallace's polemical nonfiction book *Black Macho and the Myth of the Superwoman,* in conjunction with Ntozake Shange's play *For Colored Girls* and a growing body of protest fiction by black women writers, called national attention to the conflicts in black heterosexual relationships. For the first time ever in the nation's history, television talk shows featured black women writers talking about the dynamics between black women and men. Of course none of the discussion focused on the issue of love. It was all focused on the question of power; issues like whether black women were matriarchal and castrating, holding the black man back, ruled the day. No one talked about the overall psychological impact of the rupture in black solidarity created by patriarchal thinking.

By casting black females as the "enemy," black men were essentially stating that black women were not worthy of their love and regard. And underlying this insistence on black female unworthiness was the assumption that as long as black men could not be patriarchs they could not love themselves. While all this dialogue was happening in academic and activist settings, in everyday life the vast majority of black women and men grappled with the issue of male domination. Females who wanted black male partners felt that they had to conform to sexist expectations. Tragically, where much attention had been given to heterosexual bonds of affection and love prior to these conflicts, all the attention was now focused on black male satisfaction. There was no discussion of whether or not patriarchal black men who ruled over home and family were actually emotionally fulfilled and loved.

In our patriarchal home, love for our father always took

second place to our fear of him. Growing up in a household where our mother was willingly subordinate to our father and used Christian teaching to justify female obedience to males, I witnessed firsthand the way in which male domination, like all forms of domination, makes love impossible. While one can care for someone deeply and dominate them, it is impossible to truly love someone and dominate them. Love and domination are antithetical. In *When All You've Ever Wanted Isn't Enough,* Rabbi Harold Kushner reminds us that "Love can be generated only between people who see themselves as equals, between people who can be mutually fulfilling to each other. When one commands and the other obeys, there can be loyalty and gratitude but not love." While benevolent patriarchal homes (where men rule without violent and/or abusive coercion) can be and often are households where affection and care abound, love cannot be sustained fully in any environment where the spiritual and emotional growth of any family member is not fully encouraged. Insightfully Kushner, echoing psychoanalyst Carl Jung, reminds us that love and power are not compatible: "You can love someone and give him the room and the right to be himself, or you can try to control him, to make him do your will whether for his own good or for the enhancement of your own ego. But you cannot do both at the same time." When sexist black males became obsessed with the need to exert power over black females, a barrier was created blocking our capacity to love one another.

Nowhere was a shift in black male thinking about the nature of love more evident than in black popular music. In black expressive culture, a dialogue has existed primarily in musical lyrics. Singers of every ilk, whether blues or R&B or other forms, sang about the longing to love and be loved. Popular male vocalists like Sam Cooke and Otis Redding gave voice to men's longing, their emotional vulnerability. Songs with lyrics like "Try a little tenderness," "This is my lover's prayer, I hope it reaches out to you," and the eternally popular Aretha Franklin singing, "All I am asking for is respect when I come home," voiced the emotional conflict of black males and females seeking to learn how to love. Today's popular lyrics express cynicism about love. Lust and struggles for power define the nature of black heterosexual romance. Dr. Dre, R. Kelly, and a host of other singers project hateful images of women as objects. Lyrics that say "You remind me of my Jeep" dehumanize females. In misogynistic rap music women are degraded objects, "bitches and hos." While older black folks often sit back and criticize the hatred of females these lyrics express, they do not link this misogyny to the overall insistence on the part of black leaders and many of their followers that black male patriarchy will redeem the black family. Fortunately female singers like Lauryn Hill and MeShell Ndegéocello are wonderful examples of black artists who explore love and relationships with grace, honesty, and respect.

Indeed, there is often so much discussion of "the black family," usually referring to a unit composed of adults and children, that not enough attention or value is given to the emotional relationship between black heterosexual partners. This has to do also with the legacy of slavery. Since marital unions between black men and women were devalued and couples were separated, this pattern of devaluation continued even after slavery ended and on until the present. When we read about powerful anti-racist black female leaders like Sojourner Truth, the message that comes across is that their greatest sorrow in slavery had to do with separation from children and not from the men with whom they sired those offspring. Sojourner Truth's declaration, "When I cried out in a mother's grief none but Jesus heard," poignantly expresses this lament. Yet where is the lamentation for the woundedness and brokenheartedness that has marked and marred unions between black women and men?

While courageous progressive black females, like Abbey Lincoln, offered these lamentations as part of the anti-racist, anti-sexist resistance struggle in the late sixties and early seventies, as mass movements for social justice lost momentum so did vigilant affirmative focus on black heterosexual relationships. Divorce rates, which are much higher for black couples than for other groups in this society, are one serious indication of crisis. Having had the good fortune to be raised in a small southern black community in the fifties where I saw many black couples committed to each other for life, I was disbelieving when I entered a predominately white academic world where relationships between black women and men were presented as always problematic, a world of absent fathers and lovers, of domestic strife and violence. While there were troubled relationships in the world of my growing up, the norm was black couples like my grandparents and parents, who forged lifetime commitments, staying together through thick and thin. I witnessed mutual love between black men and women throughout my childhood, and that witnessing has been vital, as it has helped me keep faith in black heterosexual love in a world where the messages received through mass media tell everyone no lasting love exists between black women and men.

Currently music videos and films created by black artists offer as problematic a vision of romantic heterosexual relationships as any vision created by mainstream white culture. Again and again black female bodies are objectified by a pornographic gaze. Black men are portrayed as desiring a woman solely on the basis of how she looks. Physical appearance is important and no one can deny that it is a factor shaping desire, but when it is the sole or most important factor determining desire or partner choice, problems arise.

Many black men are in unfulfilling relationships with women with whom they share no common interests or values because they were initially drawn solely to the way the women looked. In mass media relationships between black women and men are rarely based on shared communication. Once when I was teaching a course on black women writers I asked the more than forty black students in the classroom if they remembered their parents talking together. The vast majority of individuals could not recall open communication and/or discussion of problems. In our family my parents often talked at each other rather than with each other. Even if our father was in the same room, our mother might say to one of us children, "Tell your father." And he might do the same.

A 1992 issue of *Essence* magazine (with a picture of Malcolm X on the cover) included a story about the marriage of Betty Shabazz and Malcolm X titled "On Loving and Losing Him." One of the few black women married to a famous black leader who have ever publicly uttered even the slightest criticism of husbands, whether they are dead or alive, Shabazz shared in this piece that she subordinated her own desires and concerns to Malcolm's, acknowledging not only a lack of communication between them but that Malcolm was oftentimes controlling. Malcolm X had already revealed a misogynist bent in *The Autobiography of Malcolm X* as told to Alex Haley. Early on in his career he openly expressed conventional sexist thinking about females—that is, women are manipulative, betraying, and licentious. Shabazz shared that her husband told her before they were married that "it would be very difficult for him to tell a wife where he was, where he was going, when he was coming back," that he was driven by the "fear of a woman having control." And she confessed, "When we got married, I never asked his whereabouts."

Shabazz unwittingly shared her husband's undesirable traits even as she described the marriage in glorious terms, waxing eloquent: "I knew he loved me for my clear brown skin—it was very smooth. He liked my clear eyes. He liked my gleaming dark hair. I was very thin then, and he liked my black beauty, my mind." Of course, nothing in this piece would offer a reader who did not know about Malcolm X information about his politics, philosophy, or activism. At the same time there is no information about what was actually on Betty Shabazz's mind. We do not know from this discussion whether her political vision was similar to her husband's, whether they talked politics, and so on. Instead Shabazz outlines a very conventional sexist marriage where the husband goes out into the world and the wife stays home and takes care of the children.

It was only after her husband died that Shabazz assumed responsibility for her intellectual and political growth. Like Coretta Scott King, in her marriage she accepted being the woman behind the man, subordinated to his whims and desires. Despite widespread media coverage of Martin Luther King's sexual infidelities, his widow has never talked about the problematic nature of their marriage. Wedded to their husbands in life and death, these women became famous widows profiting from and keeping alive the legacy of the men they married. Neither Shabazz nor King married again. They never talked publicly about desiring a new relationship. Conforming to sexist notions of the dutiful wife, their experiences did not serve as a catalyst for them to assume leadership roles by offering political insights into the nature of black heterosexual bonds. Their allegiance to patriarchy stood in the way of any will to talk about the problematic nature of male domination. As black female role models they represented the status quo, even though it is evident to any researcher critically examining their lives that these marriages were not unions based on mutual communication and understanding. They were based on male domination and female subservience, like most high-profile black marriages. Can we imagine a charismatic black man never marrying again if his female partner died? But black females married to black men are expected to remain bonded, to remain loyal to his memory if the male dies.

Many black males share Malcolm X's fear of being controlled by a woman. This fear often stems from childhood experiences where mothers "smothered" their sons, using ties of affection to bind and control them. The all-giving mother who meets her son's every need tends to also seek to shape and control his actions. As a child the male may fear that any attempt to assert autonomy will cut him off from Mother's affection, so he conforms to every wish even as he may feel rage at her possessiveness. To please Mom, young black males often create a seductive false self which they use to manipulate and work around the domineering, controlling mother. The idealization of black mothers as the epitome of femininity has always made it difficult for black males either to critique their mothers (even when they are dominating and abusive) or to resist symbolically assuming the role of surrogate lover. Lots of black mothers look to their sons for the effectual engagement that is often not there between them and grown black male peers. These mothers are often afraid of losing their sons, and especially of losing their power and influence over them. To protect and keep their bond primary, they may teach the male child from an early childhood to

regard all other women negatively, to see them as destroying predators. This is emotional incest—and all incest is
abusive.

No wonder then that the mother–child paradigm often
is the one example of male–female bonding black males
have. Black males who are infantilized by overbearing
mothers who try and meet their every need often expect all
other women to do the same. When a black female partner
refuses this role, they may act out or see her as hard and
demanding. These mama's boys may grow up to desire a
woman who is just like "Mama," but they may also vent
the rage and hostility they felt over being controlled early
in life by the powerful woman/mother in adult romantic
relationships. When interracial dating became more of an
accepted norm, black males often talked about the fact
that they felt sexually free with white females because they
did not see them as being like their mothers. Most of the
black males I encounter remain reluctant to critically
examine psychoanalytically both their relationships with
their mothers and the way in which those relationships
became the model for all other relationships. Just as the
relationships with their mothers may have had a sadomasochistic push-pull dimension, this becomes the central
trait of their adult heterosexual romantic unions. Since the
will to power is always central in this type of bond, the
conditions for sustained love rarely emerge.

In so many black families, like those of other groups in
our culture, whether fathers are present or absent, relationships are seen as sites of powerful struggle where one
person is always on top. A single heterosexual female parent may feel that she must always establish her control
over home and children, letting boyfriends know that they
cannot dictate in her household. While her actions may
represent a resistance to male domination, they are an
affirmation of patriarchal lessons which teach everyone
that the home must have a "ruler"—and usually that the
one who pays the bills rules the roost. To change this
thinking collectively, black folks must begin to think of
home and heterosexual relationships as locations where
everyone's needs can be met, where there can be mutual
understanding and satisfaction. This vision of mutual love
is not one that we see in the mass media or hear high-
profile black couples talk about publicly.

There have been few marriages between black men and
women highlighted in the mass media where the emphasis
is on mutual love and partnership. For years we have been
grateful to have the example of Ruby Dee and Ossie Davis.
Initially actress Jada Pinkett spoke eloquently about mutu-
ality prior to her marriage to Will Smith and he followed
suit. Yet much of what he has conveyed about the nature
of their union since then has followed the conventional
patriarchal model. At public events he tells jokes about her

keeping him in line, constructing, however humorously, an image of her as a conventional "nagging" wife who keeps him in check. Heterosexual black males in the public eye who speak positively about marital unions with black women tend to cast their wives always in the role of either support staff (i.e., the woman behind the man who really runs the show) or maternal police (i.e., she keeps me in line). Michael Jordan and Denzel Washington are two prime examples. Again the nature of love is not discussed. This is equally true of black male intellectuals who, though not as highlighted in the mass media as movie stars and politicians, are seen as leaders shaping the actions of a black public concerned with black heterosexual bonding. Cultural critic Michael Dyson's love letter to his wife in a recent book honors her presence in a progressive way.

All too often black men say nothing about heterosexual unions between black women and men until mainstream white culture highlights a crisis. When Anita Hill testified against Clarence Thomas in the Senate hearings about his Supreme Court appointment, black men came out of the woodwork in droves to support Thomas and denounce Hill as a traitor to the race. Few black men took a public stand against sexual harassment. Likewise, when boxer Mike Tyson was accused and convicted of rape, masses of black men supported him, accusing the young woman whom he victimized of being a traitor, a manipulative whore, and so on. The same criticism can be made of the late Tupac Shakur, who always expressed love for black females but then stood by while his peers raped a young woman. All the events of the last few years which highlight heterosexual contact between black men and women reveal the pervasiveness of sexism in black communities, in the black male mind-set. It cannot be stated often enough that domination makes love impossible. Black men who embrace sexism believe it is the ability to dominate that makes them men; they choose power over love.

That sexism continues to lead black males to classify black women as madonnas or whores. The black female madonna is consistently portrayed as one who stands behind her man silently obeying his will or publicly pretending to do so, and satisfying his needs in private. The whore is always portrayed as the woman who talks too much, too loudly, who talks back, a woman who has needs of her own and is not afraid to satisfy those needs. Any black female risks being labeled a whore, whether she is sexually active or not, by sexist black men if she does not conform to their expectations of desirable femininity. Once a woman has been labeled a whore and/or bitch, it becomes possible for sexist black males to justify their abusive behavior in relation to her. In her collection of autobiographically based essays *Straight, No Chaser: How I Became a Grown-up Black Woman,* Jill Nelson recalls an evening when she is sitting at a bar next to a stranger, a drinking black male who, as she puts it, "proudly slurs" as he tells her that he does not date black women. When she asks him to explain, he shares his perception that black women are "too hard, too mean, too demanding" and "always in a man's face, got something to say about everything." Nelson responds by sharing the insight: "Maybe it's not black women you're not interested in. Maybe it's that you don't want an equal partner." With this counterpoint their discussion ends.

In her collection of essays Nelson continually calls attention to the way in which male domination and individual self-hatred make it impossible for most black males and females to know love. Analyzing mass-media devaluation of black womanhood and black manhood, she reminds us: "African-Americans, the biggest consumers of television, are those who need it least and are most harmed by it. . . . Despite the efforts of critics and activists, negative and often violent representations of black women, men, and children continue to dominate, with devastating effect. What would make us think we can watch television and then go into the real world with a positive image of, much less respect for, black women? Black People! Turn the Television OFF!" Without images of loving black folks in the mass media, all viewers, especially black audiences, are given the impression that love is not a black thing, that all our relationships are predatory, that struggles for power prevail. Even though films like *Sprung, Love Jones, Woo,* and *The Best Man* celebrate bondings between young black males and females, the behavior of the characters suggests that they are adolescents, emotionally insecure and unable to relate as mature adults.

The absence of sophisticated screen images of black heterosexual relationships is due to the combined effect of racism and sexism in both producers and consumers. Fearful of having a product that will not sell, cultural workers who have a more progressive vision often end up giving up or compromising. When a celebrated filmmaker like Spike Lee finally offered a more progressive vision of black female sexuality and black male–female interaction in the film *Girl 6,* it was trashed by critics and viewers. Audiences have to be educated to embrace more progressive images. That remains a difficult project in a world where viewers often want films to resonate with their real-life experiences. In real life most relationships between black males and females are not based on mutual respect and equality. Strife and conflict, secrets and betrayal constitute an ongoing pattern in many of these relationships, so viewers are not disturbed when this is what is portrayed on the screen. Yet until different images can be imagined in the minds of both those who produce images and those who are trying to build relationships in real life, the loving bonds we seek cannot emerge.

As long as black heterosexual relationships are primarily seen as settings for competition and struggle, love cannot become the order of the day. Many black folks, especially males, like to imagine that if all black women and men would just conform to the sexist roles assigned them, everything would be harmonious—black families would thrive. In reality, patriarchal black households where women are subservient and the male is in charge, providing and protecting, are often loveless. Love cannot prevail when one person must suppress his or her subjectivity, desires, and feelings in order to please another. And even when this does not happen, patriarchal men often still feel dissatisfied, still feel an emotional lack. They may try to fulfill that lack by seeking relationships outside their primary home, creating an atmosphere of secrecy and mistrust that ultimately erodes intimacy.

Anyone living in a traditional black community has witnessed the bourgeois patriarchal marriage where everything appears to be harmonious because all genuine feeling is repressed. It's often difficult for the powerless to imagine that seemingly powerful men can be damaged by living in a state of emotional lack, but the truth remains that males become psychologically wounded when they embrace patriarchal notions of manhood that render them unable to express feelings. Men and women alike are often depressed in these settings. That depression can be expressed by emotional withdrawal or acting out. Having affairs is the primary way dissatisfied partners act out. In their recent autobiography, *In This Life Together,* Ossie Davis and Ruby Dee share with readers the values that have helped them sustain a long and loving marriage. Speaking openly about extramarital affairs, they state: "It occurred to us, from observation and from reasoning, that extramarital sex was not what really destroyed marriages, but rather the lies and deception that invariably accompanied it."

All too often in black heterosexual relationships, dishonesty is not seen as counterproductive. Despite the longevity in most marriages between black women and men I witnessed growing up, men in those marriages regularly cheated on their wives. Conventional patriarchal assumptions about the nature of masculine sexuality justified male sexual roaming. A popular television phrase, "Have gun will travel," was translated into black vernacular as "Have dick will travel." Within traditional sexist relationships and marriages, men were not expected to be faithful. Real men proved their maleness by not remaining faithful. A faithful man was often seen as "pussy whipped." When I settled down in a long-term relationship with a black male who respected my rights and with whom I had open and honest communication, his male friends ridiculed him for being "whipped." In their minds a real man would not share his feelings and thoughts or explain his actions to a woman. After more than ten years, sexist thinking prevailed in our relationship and we parted. Though politically progressive about issues of race and class, when it came to the issue of gender, this partner, along with the majority of black males I have dated, wanted a woman whose primary reason for living was meeting his needs, particularly sexual needs.

When I chose to leave this longtime bittersweet relationship, most of the black folks in my life felt I was making a mistake. To them, ours was one of the best relationships they had ever seen between a progressive black woman and man. While we had conflicts and problems, we had handled them judiciously with counseling and open discussion. Many of these folks felt I was disappointed because I was expecting too much in the first place, expecting a black man to support gender equality both in the public sphere and in the private sphere, expecting open and honest communication—things that should be basic in a loving relationship were seen as unreasonable demands for a black male. I left this relationship and went to teach at Yale University. Hanging out with the staff who worked in African-American studies, I once had a conversation with a black woman friend who asked me to tell her what I wanted in a partner. I told her that I most wanted someone committed to open, honest communication, to processing and talking things over, especially if there was conflict. I can still remember her hearty laughter as she responded: "If that's what you want then you are not talking about being with a black male."

At that time I was thirty-five years old, living far away from the segregated black community of my growing-up years. As frightened then as I was when I entered a predominately white college on the West Coast when I was eighteen by the cynical takes on black masculinity I heard everywhere, I continued to hold in my mind and memory the images of diverse black masculinity I had known before leaving my home community. In that world I had known loving black men, witnessed them in relationships with wives, family, and community. And I persevered in my belief that loving black men exist in diverse black communities.

Honoring their presence in my life, I held and hold to the belief that black males are as capable of giving love as anyone else. Despite the problems of my first longtime primary relationship, we always communicated well. While I have been in a live-together committed relationship with only two men in my life, both black, they were both men who were willing to engage in critical dialogue and constructive exchange. Bonds of affection continue to unite us even after the relationships ended because we did process all that had happened while we were together. When problems were beyond our understanding we sought professional help.

Obviously, we live in a society that remains white supremacist, capitalist, and patriarchal. As long as these systems dominate all our lives, black people, and especially anti-sexist black couples, will always need to vigilantly create the alternative ground where our love can grow and flourish. Much of what we encounter in the mainstream culture will militate against this love. More and more black people are internalizing a negative vision of black heterosexuality. Unless we continually and collectively challenge the construction of our bonds as always and only predatory and ruthless, all signs of love between black women and men will be erased.

Representations of loving black couples, whether real or fictional, are not interesting to an American audience hungry for pathological images of black life, a hunger fueled by white supremacist thinking. As more and more black consumers internalize white supremacist thought, colluding with the dominant culture, these images increasingly come to be accepted by everyone as definitive statements about who we are and how we love. Most consumers fail to understand that any black cultural worker or producer who does not own the means of production must always

find support for a project by pitching it to white producers, most of whom are unenlightened about the way in
which racist biases shape their perceptions of black life.
There is always a small body of artistic work created
which conveys loving black bonds that may never find its
way to any public because those who market the goods
may see it as irrelevant.

Black consumers have become complacent. A movie or
book that has black characters is often hailed and celebrated no matter its quality. Trashy work by the McMillan
sisters or male author Omar Tyree are often wrongly
viewed as serious literary work. Where are our books of
love letters, our biographical and fictional narratives of
complex love relationships between black women and
men? And where is our continued support of this work
when it appears? If this work already exists in the shad-
ows, then it is our responsibility as progressive black people to bring it into the light of day. This is no simple task.
When I chose to write a memoir about my longtime relationship with a black male writer and intellectual, I
received criticism from conservative black thinkers, male
and female, who raised issues about the importance of privacy, who without even reading the book tried to suggest
it was "an attack on the brother." Ironically, had these
individuals been in power, in control of the mass media,
my book might never have been published.

To ensure the future of black heterosexual relationships we need to stop the secrets and lies. We need to talk openly about how black men and women relate, about ways class differences inform our attitudes about love, about the addiction to male domination that is strong among black men of all classes. We need to create the cultural space to talk about the love relationships we have that are fulfilling and satisfying. In some cases, we must see the sacrifice of privacy as part of the anti-racist, anti-sexist resistance struggle wherein critical vigilance requires sharing our positive and negative stories. We can only decolonize our minds, let go of the images of lovelessness that daily bombard our psyches, by erasing those images and putting in their place representations of care and affection, of black women and men bound by everlasting ties of mutual love.

*Ten*

# embracing gayness—
# unbroken circles

IN THE LATE sixties and early seventies, when black liberation was made synonymous with black men becoming patriarchs, no one talked about the way in which this uncritical support of male domination altered the nature of love in black communities. While it had a devastating impact on black heterosexual unions, it had tragic consequences for black homosexuals. Whereas tolerance of difference, including sexual difference, had been a norm in the lives of black people who had themselves been subject to genocidal assault engendered by intolerance prior to militant black power, this support changed. Patriarchal black male takeover of the civil rights struggle ushered in a mood of intolerance. With the call to dominate and control black women by any means necessary came the call to attack, crush, and if necessary kill homosexuals, especially the black male "fag." This was the term Eldridge Cleaver and his cohorts used to put down any black male who was not willing to assume a macho pose. Patriarchal black male leaders overtly expressed homophobia and encouraged other black people to join them.

Homophobia has always been a reality in black life. Hatred and fear of homosexuals was taught to many black folks by religious leaders. Prior to the sixties, black folks were much more willing to interpret scripture in ways that affirmed loving one another. Growing up in our small Kentucky town, as a family we had the good fortune to live across the street from the Smith family, an elderly couple who lived with their adult son, Mr. Richard, a schoolteacher. In those days everyone used the word "funny" to describe homosexuals. We learned at school that Mr. Richard was "funny." At home we were taught to respect him, to appreciate the way he cared for his mother and father. When I told Ms. Rosa Bell, my mother, that I was writing this chapter, we talked about why there had been this spirit of tolerance then. She shared that in small towns where black people "had known someone all their life," you accepted folks' sexuality because they were "just born that way"—"They couldn't change themselves and you could not change them, so there was no point in trying." In those days black Christian fundamentalists emphasized the importance of religious teachings that urged us to love everyone.

Growing up, we loved the gay men and women in our communities. Many of them were professionals. By today's standards they would appear closeted, because even though everyone knew that they were gay, they did not speak about it openly. It was also evident that male homosexuality was much more widely accepted than lesbianism. Black gay men in the town I grew up in adopted children, usually choosing a child from a family without the means to care for all their kin. These children always had ties of affection and interaction with their biological family, even though they stayed with their adopted kin. They did not "become" gay, nor did anyone express concern that being around gay folks would be corrupting (an expression of homophobic thinking that has now become more commonplace in black life).

The histories of black gay people in segregated communities prior to racial integration have yet to be written. Sadly, many of the voices who could have given firsthand accounts of life as it was lived then have passed away. As with all aspects of black life, urban experience often receives more attention and tends to be seen as the norm, so that often the unique experiences of black people in small towns in America are never critically examined. In interviews and conversations with black people who lived in racially segregated communities prior to the fifties, I have heard much testimony about the positive integration of gay black people into the life of black communities. Speaking about his childhood in an interview in *Sojourners*, the Reverend Carl Bean, an out gay artist and evangelist, remembers: "I was born in the '40s, raised in a time and place where the black community was very separate from the rest of society. . . . There was a feeling of family that was natural and that you were taught to be a part of. . . . And now that I look back on that kind of respect, I'm sure it all provided the foundation for what my life is today." When asked if homosexuality was accepted back then, Bean recalls, "It was a part of the community. Of course, at that time I didn't know 'gay' or anything, but I knew you could be that way in the community. So I came up with the sense that it was a part of us—it wasn't separate. That was in men. There were women who were real masculine, and everybody knew who they were, their names, and their mommies and daddies. So that base was there for me."

The spirit of tolerance in diverse segregated black communities that enabled many gay individuals to remain there and flourish even after racial interaction led to the formation of gay subcultures is rarely talked about. Southern black gay men over thirty that I spoke with who have chosen to remain in all-black conservative communities rather than shift to integrated gay subcultures feel that they would miss the experience of being a part of a larger black community, of being loved in that world despite the reality of homophobia.

Without idealizing the past, it is important for black people to remember that love was the foundation of the acceptance many gay individuals felt in the segregated communities they were raised in. While not everyone loved them or even accepted their lifestyle, there was enough affirmation present to sustain them. Since legalized racial segregation meant that black communities could not expel gay folks, those communities had to come to terms with the reality of gay people in their midst. Straight folks who had been taught by religious teachings to love everybody as oneself were compelled to create a practice of acceptance that was redemptive for both the heterosexual and the homosexual because it offered them an opportunity to, as it was common to say then, "live the faith." It is no accident that the most "out" of these gay people were often singers and musicians who first made their debut in the church. Just as the church can and often does provide a platform encouraging the denigration and ostracization of homosexuals, a liberatory house of God can alternatively be the place where all are made welcome—all are recognized as worthy. In some small segregated black communities the church was a safe house, providing both shelter and sanctuary for anyone looked upon as different or deviant, and that included gay believers.

Often gay individuals brought their talents to the church and offered them in the service of the divine. This has led some people to believe that gay people are inherently more attuned to aesthetics than others. In reality, individual homosexuals, especially black males raised in traditional black communities who did not blend in with the dominant masculinities, cultivated artistic abilities because art became a safe place as well. This is why so many of the choir directors and musicians were gay. David Hajdu's biography of the composer and musician Billy Strayhorn, *Lush Life,* documents that as a young boy Billy kept himself aloof from everyone by passionately pursuing his music. When he did reluctantly enter the accepted social scene, his special talents earned him recognition and a measure of acceptance. Everyone who knew him growing up recalls that he never showed any interest in females.

Without ambivalence, without shame or regret, Strayhorn was able to embrace his gayness. When he came to New York and fell in love with a fellow black male, he conducted their relationship with what Hajdu describes as "guileless assurance." In keeping with the self-love that had always led Strayhorn to choose situations that would further his growth, the decision to pursue working with Duke Ellington was as much a career choice as it was based on the understanding that in the Duke's milieu he could be accepted. Ellington was known for being egalitarian. Hajdu's biography shares the testimony of another gay black musician affirming the importance of Ellington's non-homophobic acceptance: "For those of us who were both black and homosexual in that time, acceptance was of paramount importance, absolute paramount importance. Duke Ellington afforded Billy Strayhorn that acceptance. That was something that cannot be undervalued or underappreciated." Ellington's ability to accept homosexuality was tied to the way he had been raised—to be appreciative of black folk, to be tolerant of those who were different, to be against domination and oppression in all their forms.

Nothing has damaged this spirit of loving kindness and tolerance in black life more than the absolute embrace of patriarchal thinking. Sixties black militants not only self-righteously attacked homosexuals, they made homophobia a criterion for authentic blackness. This was evidenced by Eldridge Cleaver's blatant attack on James Baldwin, whom he wanted to dethrone from his position as an authority and spokesperson for black experience. In an essay on Baldwin's work Cleaver called him a traitor, a puppet of the white power structure who was engaged in "a despicable underground guerilla war, waged on paper against black masculinity." Writing about Cleaver's attack on Baldwin in *Thirteen Ways of Looking at a Black Man*, Henry Louis Gates explains: "What was different this time was a newly sexualized black nationalism that could stigmatize homosexuality as a capitulation to alien white norms, and correspondingly accredit homophobia—a powerful means of policing the sexual arena—as a progressive political act." It is not surprising that at this historical moment more black people than ever before, especially the young, were turning their backs on the Christian church.

The same black macho men who attacked Baldwin by calling him Martin Luther Queen attacked King's message of love, tolerance, and forgiveness. Despite their useful critiques of racism and white supremacy, these black power advocates ushered in a wave of militant resistance which validated violence, which encouraged black people to sit in judgment of one another, to turn against one another and see one another as enemies. No wonder then that as the feminist movement launched its insightful critiques of patriarchy, black lesbian writers and thinkers were among the first group of black females to add their voices to the struggle. Poets Pat Parker and Audre Lorde were among the first black women to courageously critique patriarchy and homophobia in black life.

In her collection of essays *Sister Outsider*, Lorde remem-

bered the way homophobia was used as a weapon by sexist black men against black women activists, gay and
straight: "Today, the red herring of lesbian-baiting is being
used in the Black community to obscure the true face of
racism/sexism. Black women sharing close ties with each
other, politically or emotionally, are not the enemies of
Black men." Lorde added: "The Black Lesbian has come
under increasing attack from both Black men and heterosexual Black women. In the same way that the existence of
the self-defined Black woman is no threat to the self-
defined Black man, the Black lesbian is an emotional
threat only to those Black women whose feelings of kinship and love for other Black women are problematic in
some way. For so long, we have been encouraged to view
each other with suspicion, as eternal competitors, or as the
visible face of our self-rejection." Lorde's essays urged
black people to remember our history and to allow our
historical struggle against domination to lead us to resist
all forms of oppression. Rightly, she urged black folks to
challenge homophobia.

Loving blackness means that we love all of who we are,
and that includes gay black people. In recent years, I have
been asked by young black heterosexual militants who still
wrongly cling to the homophobia black power condoned
whether or not we "should accept gays." I remind them
that gay black people are here to stay and are not looking

to heterosexuals to validate their reality, their worth, their authenticity. Decolonized gay black people are doing the work of self-love. While it hurts when straight black people are not allies in struggle or are blatantly homophobic, the burden of change has shifted; black heterosexuals must be held accountable for homophobia and do the work of challenge and change. In a world where popular music like rap and house reinforces homophobia, this is not an easy task. It is made even harder when prominent young black people like Sister Souljah perpetuate homophobic thinking. In her book of autobiographical essays, *No Disrespect*, she describes gay lifestyles as unnatural, repeating patriarchal stereotypes about lesbian women: "Well, one of the deepest feelings a woman can experience is giving birth, the creation of life. Sex between two women cannot bring about life. It's impossible because it wasn't meant to be." Writing about a woman friend's lesbianism, Souljah is dismissive and judgmental: "I continued to feel that Mona's embrace of a lesbian life was due more to inner weakness and her victimization as a black woman than out of any genetic compulsion."

There are many reasons individuals are gay. Some folks feel they are living out a preordained biological determination and others may feel that they are making a choice. Homophobic hatred of gay people encourages heterosexuals to feel they have the right to determine the legitimacy of any person's sexual identification. These assaults on the integrity of any aspect of black experience must end if we are to reawaken the incredible spirit of tolerance and loving kindness that is our legacy—handed down to us by ancestors who out of their suffering learned the power of compassion.

Judging one another as traitors based on sexual preferences has been the easiest way to discount and dismiss the work of black people who have given or give their all to the black liberation struggle. When Angela Davis opposed the Million Man March, her detractors chose to focus on sexuality. The accusation of "lesbian" was thrown out and made synonymous with her being a traitor to the race. No matter what her sexual preference, any time an empowered black woman challenges black male patriarchal leadership, her sexuality will come under attack. When Angela Davis openly acknowledged her lesbianism in the February 1998 issue of *Out* magazine, conservative black male leaders did not even respond. But no doubt the next time they wish to discredit her politics they will refer to this magazine to prove that she is not "authentically" black-identified.

Like Davis, I opposed the march on the political grounds that it was pro-capitalist, imperialist, and patriarchal. Discussing this opposition in my Harlem classroom, I was stunned when students referred to Angela Davis as a traitor to the race, evoking lesbianism as the force fueling her treachery. At that point in time Davis had not yet spoken publicly about her sexual preferences. First I challenged students to remember all the work Davis has done and is doing on behalf of black liberation. I spoke about her time in prison, about the death threats she still receives, and asked my students if anyone present in our class had done as much for the cause of civil rights. Then I questioned their willingness to disrespect her activism, her sacrifices, by acting as though they could dismiss a political action on her part as treachery on the basis of gossip about her sexuality. I then asked the class if they had heard rumors that both Malcolm X and Martin Luther King had sexual experiences with men. They knew these rumors but did not use them to invalidate their politics, their activism. Clearly, black women were judged by a different standard.

Angela Davis has not publicly addressed the relationship between liberation politics and her sexual preferences. Even though her picture is on the cover of the issue of *Out* magazine wherein she shares this information, she does not explain in the interview her reasons for disclosing her sexual practice at this point in time. Readers are told, "She's no more interested in discussing her romantic life as a lesbian than she was in having her prison affair with George Jackson trotted out to prosecutors in the '70s." Of course her love affair with George Jackson was made public and was used as a platform to encourage other black women to become involved in radical militant struggle against racism. No doubt her acknowledgment that she is a lesbian will publicly impact the struggle for black gay rights.

Many prominent black women thinkers, writers, and activists are gay. Sometimes it is important for the public to know this information so that the negative stereotypes which imply that black gay people are only concerned about sexuality can be effectively challenged and debunked. Collectively the straight black world should acknowledge the powerful positive contribution of gay folks to the black liberation struggle. Such acknowledgment is always an act of resistance; it stands as a challenge to homophobia, to those who think heterosexual black folks have more rights in "blackness" than anyone else. As early as 1978, the writer June Jordan in her essay "Where Is the Love" challenged black folks to remember that sexuality does not determine or necessarily reflect politics. Lots of gay people are politically conservative. Being gay does not make one radical any more than womanizing heterosexual black men are radicalized by their sexual practice. Jordan shares: "When I speak of Black feminism I am not speaking of heterosexuality or lesbianism or homosexuality or bisexuality; whatever sexuality anyone elects for his or her pursuit is not my business, nor the business of the state. And furthermore, I cannot be persuaded that one kind of sexuality, as against another, will necessarily provide for the greater happiness of the two people involved. I am not talking about sexuality, I am talking about love; about a steady-state deep caring and respect for every other human being, a love that can only derive from a secure and positive self-love." Paradoxically, the foundation of the love Jordan describes can only be present in black life if we respect everyone's sexuality.

Indeed, one of the most destructive aspects of homophobia, in the culture as a whole and in black life in particular, is its erosion of the ground of self-love that is so necessary for the building of positive self-esteem. Given pervasive homophobia, all young black gay individuals living in diverse black communities are at risk. They risk their self-esteem being assaulted daily by a straight world that wishes to deny them equal access to a complex humanity and an array of choices about how to live and act in the world. In the autobiography of Bill T. Jones, *Last Night on Earth*, he poignantly describes the inner struggle he experienced as he endeavored to explore his sexuality, to find out its nature and then later to share with his family his preference. One of his older brothers had told him, "It's just a phase you're going through." Sharing his choice with siblings before talking to his parents, Jones felt fear and dread when his mother demanded, "What you doin' sleepin' with a man?" His father responded by addressing his wife: "Sweet, let the boy do what he's gonna do. He's a man." This confessional moment was not nearly as difficult as those of black homosexuals who are bitterly rejected by black families.

Rejecting others because one does not approve of their sexual preference is wrong-minded and downright cruel. In conversation with one of my sisters I made reference to our lesbian sister. She stressed that she could not condone homosexuality, that the Bible labeled it a sin. I pointed out to her that the Bible labeled adultery a sin, but she did not ostracize and punish either her partner or the other adulterers in her life. When it suited her needs as a heterosexual she would interpret the Bible in a more progressive manner. Yet she used it to reinforce her fear of homosexuality. A similar strategy is used by gay-hating Christians. This is tragic.

Loving black families make a space where each individual family member can self-actualize, can embrace their sexuality as it evolves. Were more black people willing to let go of the patriarchal mind-set that stands in the way of love, homophobia could be effectively challenged and eradicated in our communities. Black gay men have been the group of males at the forefront of anti-sexist efforts in black life. My now-deceased comrade and friend the poet Essex Hemphill fiercely critiqued patriarchal thinking and male domination wherever it surfaced among gay or straight black men. When he met my black male partner for the first time, he took him aside to talk with him, to make sure, he told him, "that you understand how to respect and love this black woman." Though taken aback, my partner welcomed this gesture of protective love. This gesture, like so many others that Hemphill made in his life, shattered the negative stereotype that gay men only compete with women and do not care about our emotional well-being. Many individual black women would know no love from black males if it were not for the emotionally fulfilling bonds of care established with non-sexist, loving black gay men. Gay men who buy into patriarchal thinking are just as sexist as their straight counterparts. In a discussion with black filmmaker Isaac Julien, who is also gay, Hemphill states: "Think about the things you have heard among gay brothers about women. How much different are some of those statements from the ones by some heterosexual brothers. . . . I don't think current definitions of masculinity work for any male. I don't think they work for anyone." Gay men were often annoyed when Hemphill challenged them to critique their sexism. His willingness to challenge the patriarchy, even in situations where it made him unpopular, was a way of expressing both his self-love and his love for black womanhood.

When he was alive, Marlon Riggs, activist, scholar, and filmmaker, used to insist in conversations with me and

Essex that "black men loving black men was the most revolutionary act." To Marlon this statement was an affirmation of the importance of self-love. He believed that a
self-hating individual black male, irrespective of his sexual
preference, would never be able to love another black
male. While I agree that anyone mired in self-hate cannot
love anyone, I used to tell him that the "most revolutionary act" black men could make was to deal psychoanalytically with their childhoods. For it is in childhood that so
many black males, gay and straight, come to fear masculinity and manhood. This fear is often based on painful
and abusive interaction between fathers and/or male
parental caretakers and sons.

Longtime gay activist Joseph Beam was one of the first
out black men to seriously address the issue of heterosexual black male and gay black male interaction, particularly
the relationships between fathers and sons. Writing about
his own father, whom he experienced as kind and gentle,
Beam states, "We are silent when alone together. . . . Our
love for each other, though great, may never be spoken. It
is the often unspoken love that Black men give to other
Black men in a world where we are forced to cup our hands
over our mouths or suffer under the lash of imprisonment,
unemployment, or even death. But these words, which fail,
are precisely the words that are life-giving and continuing.
They must be given voice." Fear of homosexuality has led

many black adult men to withhold their love from male children and adult peers. Rooted in homophobia, this fear must be overcome if black men are to experience self-love. At the same time, until black folks openly address same-sex incest, the sexual abuse of black boys by older males, self-love will not become the norm for all black men.

Self-loving black men do not fear being gay. For they know that embracing their sexuality, in whatever form it takes, is a gesture of self-acceptance necessary to love. Recently the resurgence of patriarchally based Afrocentric black nationalism has given rise to unprecedented forms of gay-bashing in black communities. It has shocked me to hear black males and females boast that they would kill a child of theirs who was gay. These genocidal impulses are the outcome of homophobia run amok. They are linked to misogynist woman-hating. The prevalence of homophobia in all our lives assaults the integrity of the entire black body politic. For a people whose bodies have been subjected to all manner of torture and degradation, who have been persecuted on the basis of our skin color, over which we have no control, the foundation of our survival with our humanity intact has been our willingness to challenge domination. We can never ensure the safety of our freedom to self-actualize if we do not wish to claim those rights for everyone, including our gay brothers and sisters.

There is no black person who does not have a gay relative somewhere in the family tree. Often when family members foolishly indulge in homophobic jokes and verbal gay-bashing, they assume that the gay person is a stranger, someone out there whom they will never know. The gay person is always with us—inside the home, a part of our family. If their presence is not known to everyone it is usually because the environment is not a safe and affirming atmosphere to be openly out in. Most black folks care for someone who is gay without knowing their sexual preference. That space of unknowing can be the space where heterosexuals hurt and wound our gay relatives. When heterosexual family members create a safe and loving environment, one where judgment of value and worth is not based on sexual preference, gay individuals can dare to speak their truths, share who they truly are, give and receive the love that we all need to be fully self-actualized.

Sadly, the prevalence of HIV and AIDS in black communities has broken the walls of denial and forced many black families and communities to confront the reality that gay people and bisexual people live with and among us. In some cases individuals respond to this reality by acts of cruelty and hate, often shunning those who suffer. Indeed, until black people learn to accept that we have diverse sexualities, the sick and suffering among us will not be given the loving care that everyone deserves. Patriarchal homophobic thinking has led many black people to see the AIDS virus as punishment for wrongdoing. Such thinking is rooted in hate. It can only be challenged by acts of love. Narrow-minded black folks need to stop acting as though only straight people who are HIV-positive are worthy of care. Without an open, compassionate response to homosexuality, black folks will never be able to cope with HIV-related disease and AIDS in our communities, or understand why black women are disproportionately represented among the sick and dying. If we love each other and embrace our diverse sexualities, we create an environment where there is no sexuality that cannot speak its name. Doing this, we diminish the risk that individuals will be victimized even as we create a loving environment where gay brethren suffering with the disease can know care, can find love.

Creating communities of blackness where love and respect for diversity could be valued was an important act of resistance for newly freed black slaves. That abiding solidarity which welcomes everyone and allows them to be at home was taught to many of us in the segregated communities of our childhood. As an oppositional survival strategy it enabled the building of bonds of affection among those who were different. The desire to build communities where everyone, straight and gay, would be safe was central to the project of visionary black liberation struggle. It is this vision we must return to if we want to make our communities places where gay people can mingle and thrive, fulfilled by the knowledge that "we are family." For self-loving straight black folks, to value gay brothers and sisters as we value ourselves is a lesson in love that can redeem us all. Recognizing the love healthy gay males and females offer each other and us all is vital to loving blackness. It allows us to establish communities where no one is excluded or discriminated against. It enables us to value one another rightly, to appreciate our preferences, and to let love guide us to the place where we are made one body in love.

## Eleven

# loving justice

REDEMPTIVE LOVE HAS always had a special meaning for African-Americans. Historically, it was often thought of in terms of the boundless love of a divine will powerful enough to enable the oppressed and exploited to find their way to freedom, to survive, and to triumph. When Martin Luther King galvanized African-Americans as no other leader had ever done before, calling us to love justice above all else, in such a way that we would be willing to give our lives to be free, he demanded that we move beyond the world of politics into a transcendent spiritual place of meaningful sacrifice. This call to sacrificial love was different from the notion of loving God as a balm soothing the hurts of unjust torture and suffering. It was different from the Christian notion of forgiving and loving one's enemies. It was a call to stand for justice and freedom with one's whole heart, body, mind, and spirit.

How quickly generations of African-Americans have forgotten this legacy. Luckily a marvelous film series, *Eyes on the Prize*, lets current generations be a witness to this love. I stand in awe every time I see the footage of black folks ready to be beaten, to perhaps even lose their lives, for justice. I stand in awe gazing at the white folks who stand by their side ready to die for justice. When three men I did not know, Chaney, Goodman, and Schwerner, were murdered because they loved justice, I was twelve years old. Yet I held in my mind's eye the image of three young men, two northerners, one southerner, two white guys and one black, all in their twenties, arrested on June 21, 1964, in Mississippi and never seen again until their bodies were found. Chaney beaten, then shot; Goodman and Schwerner killed by one shot. At the service for Goodman in New York, Rabbi Arthur Lelyveld, who had gone to Mississippi once and been attacked, eulogized these young men, telling the world: "Theirs is the way of love and constructive service." They died for justice.

As a teenage girl growing up in a world that was swiftly moving from the racial apartheid I had known all my life (a separation that had erected a wall of hatred on the white side so intense it generated in us a white heat of fear) toward a desegregated world, I understood the power of justice and the meaning of sacrifice. I wondered then as I have wondered throughout my life whether or not my love of justice, that inheritance handed down to me, and to us all, by the sacrifices of anti-racist activists like Chaney, Goodman, and Schwerner, would give me the courage to offer my life—to face death. Many black freedom fighters like James Chaney were motivated to struggle and fight for justice by a courage they had learned as children in the church. They hoped to embody in word and deed the radical love of God. It was that love that would hold and sustain them in the hour of their trial, before their crucifixion—when there would be no one to bear witness.

There is a distinct difference between the outlook of black folks born and raised during periods of violently maintained segregation and the outlook of younger generations who have never really known what it was like to be excluded from schools, hospitals, and lunch counters solely on the basis of skin color. A generation of black people who have never known what it feels like to do backbreaking work on the land, to pick cotton or sharecrop, to work all day and still be hungry at night because the pay you receive for your labor cannot begin to meet your most basic everyday needs for food, clothing, and shelter, cannot experientially comprehend the extreme acts of injustice perpetrated in the name of white supremacy. Most importantly, these new generations have no sense of what it was like to live in a world of racial apartheid where the mere crossing of a boundary by look, word, or deed could lead to death. This generation is often rightfully angry because its members do not have equal access to the top spheres of power and privilege—to the best, highest-paying jobs. But they have no lived experience of what it was like to be unable to find work no matter what your level of intelligence, skill, or need. This generation has not known hunger that goes unappeased, torture that is unrelenting, fear so great it takes away your voice and renders you powerless. Right now this generation, like our nation as a whole, does not love justice.

When militant young black men embraced patriarchal thinking and decided they would walk away from a freedom struggle rooted in a love ethic and put in its place a movement based on power struggle, one advocating violence and courting death, they did not foresee that such action would place them in immediate collusion with the oppressive system they hoped to change. We need a progressive, transformative vision of social justice that would combine the wisdom of a successful nonviolent, love-based freedom struggle with the insights of a direct-action, decolonizing movement for black self-determination and liberation. While much good came from both the nonviolent civil rights movement and the more militant black power struggle for liberation, in the end the love ethic which had been so central to black survival had been discarded.

The assassination of the great prophet of love Martin Luther King, the visionary who had held out to the world the hope of ending domination through nonviolent resistance, created the context for hopelessness and despair. And it was even more a blow to the spirit of those who fought for freedom and justice when Malcolm X, who had done so much to turn young black people away from King's message, was assassinated just at that moment when he had begun to turn away from a philosophy of kill-or-be-killed toward a vision of strategic struggles for freedom grounded in both a love ethic and the will to choose self-determination. Malcolm X was not murdered at the height of his power, of his call for militant armed struggle. Despite the hype which suggests otherwise, a militaristic, imperialist, white supremacist nation wholeheartedly committed to colonizing the world "by any means necessary" understood fully that if violence was the order of the day the state would always prevail. He became much more a threat to the state when he began to oppose imperialism and critique violence as the only possible means of intervention.

Both Martin Luther King and Malcolm X were assassinated at the point when they began to hone a truly revolutionary vision of liberation, one rooted both in a love ethic and the will to resist domination in all its forms. Martin and Malcolm did not live long enough to fully integrate the love ethic into a vision of political decolonization that would offer practical guidelines for the eradication of black self-hatred, as well as strategies for building a diverse beloved community. In the essay "Love as the Practice of Freedom," I described the way in which the loss of these two visionary leaders (as well as the deaths of liberal white leaders who were our allies in the struggle for racial justice) truly devastated African-Americans.

No work has been done that examines in an in-depth manner the extent to which the loss of our leaders created major mental-health problems for black people, whose wounded morale had been sustained and rejuvenated under their loving guidance. We heard individuals openly offering testimony about the way in which news of the death of King and/or Malcolm shocked and traumatized them. Yet we did not have a mental-health community ready to confront that trauma to help us recover. Theorizing about this pain in my essay, I wrote: "Wounded in that space where we would know love, black people collectively experienced intense pain and anguish about our future. The absence of public spaces where that pain could be articulated, expressed, shared meant that it was held in—festering, suppressing the possibility that this collective grief would be reconciled in community even as a way to move beyond it and continued resistance would be envisioned. Feeling as though 'the world had come to an end,' in the sense that a hope had died that racial justice would become the norm, a life-threatening despair took hold in black life." While privileged classes of black people assuaged their feelings of loss by swift assimilation into the values of the dominant white mainstream, the black masses were left emotionally stuck. Following the path chosen by their privileged counterparts, holding to suspicion and hostility, they nevertheless began to embrace the values of white supremacist capitalist patriarchy. This created an unprecedented context for collusion in their own oppression and exploitation. It set the stage for the takeover of poor black communities by a drug economy which brought in its wake a hedonistic ethos of violence, consumerism, and amoral pursuit of pleasure powerful enough to usurp and destroy the foundations of communalism, a love ethic, and a belief in the healing power of forgiveness, faith, and compassion.

The greatest testament to the lovelessness that has taken over diverse black communities is the constant presence of meaningless, brutal, and senseless violence. As with all communities in a culture of domination, there has always been violence in black neighborhoods. Yet it has only been in the last twenty or more years that random genocidal

assault and sadomasochistic torture has become so commonplace as to not even merit comment, let alone outrage.
Since so many privileged-class black individuals live far
away from these "war zones," there is no sense of
accountability to the lifestyles of those black folks who are
stuck in lower-middle-class or poor neighborhoods ravaged by predators. The indifference of the conservative
black professional class finds extreme expression in critics
like Stanley Crouch who advocate full-scale legalized
slaughter and/or a legalized death penalty for the predatory individuals who make these neighborhoods mini-
empires where they exercise autocratic rule.

While black male leaders (all of whom have material
privilege) usually denounce predatory violence among the
underclass, the vast majority support imperialism and militarism. Evidently, they see no moral conflict between their
critique and disavowal of connection to those black males
who violently prey on black communities and those black
males who in the service of the nation-state prey on disad-
vantaged communities globally. Nation of Islam leader
Louis Farrakhan, brought to world fame by the white
supremacist, capitalist, patriarchal press, has much in
common with the white religious and political right. He
supports militarism, capitalism, imperialism, and patriarchy. He dissents from their views only on the question of
white supremacy.

In his essay "Farrakhan and the Failure of Black American Leadership," published in the anthology *The Farrakhan Factor,* Ron Nixon reports that a *Time* magazine poll showed that more than half of young black people see him as a role model. They believe he, more than any other black male leaders, addresses relevant issues, offering what Nixon calls a vision that suits the present situation: "That vision is grounded in black nationalism and the tough realities of life for many in the black community. Yet, like the visions offered by traditional black civil rights leaders and conservatives, it is a vision that fails to address the critical needs of the next generation of African-Americans—hip-hop and otherwise—who will bear the brunt of the black community's continuing deterioration." The nation-state affirmed Farrakhan's leadership when the government supported the Million Man March he spearheaded. Any scholar who studies the mission statement and the speeches given at the march will find that the primary political content of the march rests on its unequivocal support of patriarchy, capitalism, militarism, and imperialism. Love was rarely mentioned either at the march or in commentary about the march. The failure to address the transformative power of love makes sense given the central focus on domination.

As long as black leaders wrongly encourage black men, and all black people, to believe our collective wounds can be healed by the establishment of black patriarchal rule, we are doomed. For embracing patriarchy has different consequences for the black male who sits in a boardroom and the black man who must prove his masculinity on embattled ghetto streets or in the war zone of contemporary prisons. Just as some black nationalist leaders ignore the reality of diversity in our lives, of racial mixing on the job and elsewhere, and socialize black folks to embrace a narrow-minded racial separatism, more and more Afrocentric utopian fantasies are spun in literature and in popular cultural commodities which perpetuate the idea that all whites are the enemy. For some time now this has led individual black people to act as though white folks can never be our allies in struggle, can never be anti-racist. Of course embracing this wrong-minded way of thinking leads individual black folks to reject white allies in struggle who are able to assist us in dismantling white supremacy. A prime example of the way this thinking is detrimental occurs in school systems all around the nation. Black children in educational systems where they are taught by white teachers falsely assume that they are engaging in some meaningful act of resistance when they refuse information teachers offer, when they mock, ridicule, and in some cases terrorize their teachers.

Yet it is obvious who suffers the consequences of the failure to engage in an effective learning environment.

When black parents teach their children to reject all forms of knowledge coming from a white source, they betray their interests. Not only do they encourage a narrow-minded approach to human interaction in a diverse world, they ensure that their children will be ill-prepared for employment in that world. While we are right as black citizens to challenge and critique white supremacist biases in education, it does not serve the interests of black students to convince them that they have nothing to learn from anyone who is white. This cynicism about the capacity of white people to support anti-racist struggle is a cruel mockery of the history of civil rights. It denies the incredible gift offered us by anti-racist white people who have sacrificed time, safety, prestige, and in some cases their lives in the struggle to end white supremacy.

To a grave extent, contemporary demonization of all white people by individual black leaders is psychoanalytically an inversion of racialized self-hatred. The evidence supporting this fact lies with the fate of many militant black leaders, like Huey Newton and Eldridge Cleaver, who showed by their confused allegiances that they had not fully decolonized their minds. A black person who is mired in self-hatred will not be able to see the differences between a hardened white supremacist and a progressive anti-racist white person who opposes domination in all its forms.

No black male leader has ever made ending black self-hatred a primary agenda of the black liberation struggle. More often than not King highlighted the importance of loving our enemies when he placed love on the agenda. He did this in part because he had the foresight to realize that white supremacy would never be eradicated unless white people experienced a conversion experience which would show them what it meant to be just in one's actions. Since he, like many of us, had seen black people embody the love ethic in its highest ideals, he believed we were collectively ordained to set an example of the meaning of forgiveness.

Even though many progressive young black people grew to be suspicious of King's focus on forgiving our enemies (and I was one of them) because he did not talk about self-determination and self-love, we did not abandon our understanding of the reality that one gained insight through redemptive suffering, that one of the primary gains for black people lay in the practice of compassion. To show compassion for one's enemies, to be able to love them, meant that one would necessarily need to be rooted in self-love. As I study King's writings today it seems that he did not focus on self-love because he truly believed that black people were doing the work of self-love. In his short lifetime he did not seem to fully grasp the depths of the black colonized mind, of black self-hatred.

Focusing on the power of forgiveness, King also often

overlooked the importance of accountability. For genuine forgiveness to be transformative, white people undergoing a conversion process by which they divest themselves of white supremacist thinking would necessarily have to focus on accountability and atonement. Having also abandoned a love ethic when it comes to the issue of social justice, most unenlightened white citizens respond with rage at the suggestion that the nation must atone to its black citizens for the unique genocidal assaults experienced in the past and present day. Every white person who has committed themselves to anti-racist struggle understands that there is no shame to be had in assuming accountability for the collective wrong done black people by the agents of white supremacy, most of whom have been and are white. Indeed, assuming responsibility and accountability empowers.

When popular New Age guru Marianne Williamson wrote the insightful book *The Healing of America,* urging the citizens of this nation to atone for the wrongs of white supremacy, it did not receive the widespread acclaim given all her other works. Uniting the spiritual with the political in this work, Williamson calls for a return to a love ethic that would re-inspire all our nation's citizens to be concerned with ending racism and all other forms of domination. Persuasively arguing this point, she shares: "There are those who would point to blacks who have behaved

criminally or dysfunctionally, and try to use that as a justi-
fication for not performing our ethical duty toward the
African-American community. Or, conversely, one can
point to black stars who have triumphed, and try to claim
that because they have made it big in America, that proves
there's no real problem. But neither argument is valid.
Every group of people has its shadow element, and every
group of people has its geniuses. Neither is an excuse for
failing to do what needs to be done." Drawing on the
work of Martin Luther King, throughout her book
Williamson echoes his insight that a love ethic is the only
foundation for transformative renewal of ourselves and
our nation.

Progressive visionary leaders have always known that
any action which liberates and renews oppressed and
exploited black people strengthens the nation as a whole.
Not only do these actions provide a model for ending
racism, they provide strategies for the overall healing of
America. By focusing solely on the negative examples of
nihilistic, corrupt, predatory black "gangstas," white conservatives hope to strip black people of the legacy which
made us a moral vanguard. By focusing more on the personal flaws of leaders both past and present, this same
group effectively deflects attention away from the wisdom
teachings these leaders provided that would enable us to
care for the souls of black folks and the nation as a whole.

More and more, a cynical perspective abounds which perpetuates the notion that there is a dearth of black leadership, that black people lack redemptive guidelines for the saving of our souls and our diverse black communities. This is all false. Visionary black leaders abound in our society; many of them are women. Patriarchal thinking blocks recognition of the power of female wisdom and our words. Contemporary black women leaders know that we can only heal the crisis in our diverse black communities by returning to a love ethic which stands in opposition to all forms of domination, including white supremacy and sexism. Before us, visionary black thinkers, many of them women, have prepared a feast, one that can heal our souls. All things are ready, black folks have only to come. It will be pure tragedy if sexist thinking combined with internalized racism keeps individuals from partaking of all the wise teachings that offer us a path to healing and salvation.

It is no accident that just as visionary anti-sexist black women were finding a voice and making that voice heard, the dominant culture renewed its focus on patriarchal masculinity. White supremacist, capitalist, patriachal leaders know who benefits most from the disrespect and devaluation of black female wisdom. Unlike the male leaders of the past who shaped the direction of the black liberation struggle, anti-sexist thinkers, female and male, know that we must live what we preach, embodying in our habits of being the liberation we lay claim to for our collective body politic. Were our black leaders in the past and/or present fundamentally anti-patriarchal, black people would be in a different place today. We would be celebrating the oppositional spirit of solidarity and equality, communalism, and love of justice that has been our legacy.

That legacy has not been forgotten. Unrecognized visionaries stand ready to pass the torch and rekindle the flame of liberation struggle rooted in a love ethic. Money alone will never heal the wounds of black America. As long as white supremacy remains the order of the day, we must always work to control our representations, to offer a progressive vision. Returning to love and a love ethic can provide every black person with the strength to survive with dignity and passion, no matter what their economic lot in life. It can empower us to create communities of resistance that can eliminate all forms of violence in our neighborhoods: the violence of addiction, of physical abuse, of emotional torture. The resources to heal our wounds are already at our disposal. We simply need to garner the means of distribution to take action in every way. Simple things like ceasing to watch television, refusing mindless consumption, engaging in positive thinking, learning how to read and write, and learning how to think critically are among the myriad ways we can practice love in action, a redemptive love that can heal wounded spirits.

Martin Luther King offered a visionary insight when he stated: "Our goal is to create a beloved community, and this will require a qualitative change in our souls as well as a quantitative change in our lives." The individuals who are part of that beloved community are already in our lives. We do not need to search for them. We can start where we are. We begin our journey with love, and love will always bring us back to where we started. Making the choice to love can heal our wounded spirits and our body politic. It is the deepest revolution, the turning away from the world as we know it, toward the world we must make if we are to be one with the planet—one healing heart giving and sustaining life. Love is our hope and our salvation.

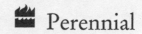 WILLIAM MORROW    Perennial

# The bell hooks Love Trilogy

### ALL ABOUT LOVE: *New Visions*
ISBN 0-06-095947-9 (paperback)

This visionary and accessible book offers radical new ways to think about love and challenges the prevailing notion that romantic love is more important than all other bonds. In thirteen concise chapters, hooks explains how our everyday notions of what it means to give and receive love often fail us, and how these ideals are established in early childhood.

"[*All About Love*] is a warm affirmation that love is possible and an attack on the culture of narcissism and selfishness." — *The New York Times Book Review*

### SALVATION: *Black People and Love*
ISBN 0-06-095949-5 (paperback)

An exploration of the roles love plays in the lives of African Americans – spanning the days of slavery to freedom, and re-narrating the liberation, civil rights and hip-hop movements. Told from both historical and cultural perspective, hooks combines both cultural critique and an emphasis on self-help and self-recovery, offering new visions that will heal our nation's wounds from a culture of lovelessness.

"A manual for fixing our culture...In writing that is elegant and penetratingly simple." — *Black Issues Book Review*

### COMMUNION: *The Female Search for Love*
ISBN 0-06-621442-4 (hardcover)

*Communion* challenges every female to courageously claim the search for love as the heroic journey she must choose to be truly free. hooks explores the ways ideas about women and love were changed by the feminist movement, by women's full participation in the work force, and by the culture of self-help. She celebrates experiences of women over 30, shares collective wisdom, and lessons learned as we practice the art of loving

"When truth teller and careful writer bell hooks offers a book, I like to be standing at the bookshop when it opens." — Maya Angelou

**Available wherever books are sold, or call 1-800-331-3761 to order.**